W9-BAM-506

ON MAKING OFF

Randy Anderson

Cover Illustrations by Chad Crowe

ON MAKING OFF
Copyright © 2011 Randy Anderson
All rights reserved.
ISBN-10: 1461041686
ISBN-13: 978-1461041689

For Scott

CONTENTS

Part IV   DO IT!

Part V   STOPPING THE WORLD

ACKNOWLEDGMENTS

Thanks to Lorraine Shea for patiently editing and encouraging, Chad Crowe for drawing my life on the cover, and Elizabeth Miller for laying it all out so well. And a special thanks to the long list of wonderfully creative theatrical collaborators who've put their asses on the line with me over the years. It is with this story that I honor your energy and spirit.

Part I
NEW YORK

LISTEN TO YOUR CORE

I like to make theater. I always have. Once, in the fifth grade, I turned a jungle gym into a walk-through haunted house and enlisted dozens of kids to be ghouls. We constructed a maze with our jackets and sent buskers out to the playground to drum up an audience. Nobody told me how to do all this. I just did it because it made me happy. I didn't know it when I was 10, but I do know it now. Making theater makes me happy.

I'm usually pretty good at beginnings. Endings give me more trouble. For me, beginnings are easy to generate. I find a place to start, create an engaging hook, and then work like mad—until I find myself looking for an ending. That's where I get into trouble. I suppose if I knew the ending, I could just as easily create a good beginning and work like mad toward that ending. But this isn't just about making theater. It's about making a life. And the best part about life is that we don't know the ending. So, we'll leave the ending to chance and just get on with it.

This story begins in Los Angeles, 18 months after my college graduation. From the backyard of the house I shared with some friends, I watched our neighbors film a poolside porn scene as I slurped my bowl of spaghetti with meat sauce. I couldn't actually see much through the slats of the wooden fence, but I could hear enough to give my imagination fodder. This was far more entertaining than daytime television.

I'd taken the day off from my "day job" at a stock-footage company to work on my acting career, which I would describe as stalled—but that would infer it had been, at some point, moving. So, I focused an entire day each week on getting my career on track. It had been a difficult year and a half. I was having a lot of trouble getting a foothold in the City of Angels and had begun questioning my decision to move there. Happiness seemed as elusive as my acting career.

After finishing my spaghetti, I jumped into my Nissan Sentra, cranked the AC, and drove down Santa Monica Boulevard in the oppressive mid-day sun.

The sun is not my friend. I'm a quarter northern Italian, a quarter Swedish, a quarter English (by way of Virginia), and a quarter... Detroit. While the flexibility of my "day job"—cooped up in a cold, windowless room watching sunsets, moonrises, and time-lapse urban panoramas over and over—did not make up for the lousy pay and monotony, at least it kept me out of the sun.

I stopped at the theater I worked at to drop off my dues check. A year before, I had auditioned for, and been accepted by, a theater company in Hollywood. Since then, I'd produced two shows, built a set for another, and ushered practically every weekend—all for the bargain price of $35 a month. And no, they weren't paying *me*. That is what I was paying *them.* They had yet to invite me to audition for a show, though my time was coming, they assured me.

This theater company was really more of a club than a theater company, but I'm a joiner. It gave me a sense of community, which was a bit difficult to find in the suburban sprawl of L.A. After calculating a quick cost/benefit analysis in my head, I dropped the envelope through the knee-high mail slot and got back into my car.

This wasn't how I imagined my life after college. As someone who hates car culture, I never pictured myself pulling into a gas station. Since I'd never owned a television set, scanning stock footage wasn't exactly my ideal profession. And I never envisioned paying a monthly fee for the potential privilege of performing with a theater company that used me for free labor. People were supposed to be paying *me*. Wasn't that the point of getting a college degree?

In my mind, I'd be performing on stage, not taking tickets at the door. Afterwards, I'd be wearing a black peacoat, taking one last drag off a cigarette, and then joining my cast mates in an Irish pub to celebrate our success. In my mind, I'd be running through New York City, having one wild adventure after another. But instead—out of fear, I suppose—I chose to get lost in a maze of freeways, search for exterior office building shots in a windowless office, and watch backyard porn shoots through the slats of a fence.

My next stop was an appointment with Patty, my agent of six months. Patty was a chain-smoking, Diet Coke–drinking, raspy-voiced broad, with a slightly collapsed '60s hairdo. She was right out of central casting—and a little slow to ramp up my career. She sent me on a couple of auditions a month, usually for crime-show re-enactments or minor commercials. Although people told me that going on a couple of auditions a month was good, I didn't believe them. I'd discovered that L.A. folks would tell you anything, so I believed nothing. I pulled into Ralph's, picked up a six-pack of Diet Coke, and headed over the hill.

Patty's single-room office was buried deep inside a converted apartment complex, which was buried deep inside the cleft of a hill, which was located just outside the right side of town. She had no receptionist and no staff, save for an occasional intern I'd see darting from her office. Stacks of headshots, piled waist-high on the floor, exposed parts of a carpet that looked like it hadn't been cleaned in years. Her desk was littered with yellow Post-its and shards of paper peppered with indecipherable scribble.

"Come in! Have a seat," Patty invited. "How can I help you?" She always sounded busy, though I never heard her phone ring.

"I'm Randy," I said, pausing at her blank expression. "Randy Anderson." She remained silent, but I could see her mind working. "One of your clients. I brought you some Diet Coke."

"Oh, yes, Randy. Thank you very much!"

I always brought her Diet Coke. It was her mnemonic for me.

"Would you like a cigarette?" she offered, as if it were a quid pro quo. She placed a Virginia Slim in her mouth and lit it. I noticed two cigarettes still burning in the ashtray.

"No thanks, I'm cutting back," I lied. I loved smoking, but what was the point of lighting up with the smoke of three cigarettes already filling the room?

"So, what can I do for you today?" she asked, as she futilely rifled through her desk to find my information.

"Well, I'm concerned about the lack of auditions you're sending me on, and I'd like to maybe think of some ways we can change that."

A true passive-aggressive, I spoke these words to her back as she bent over, looking for my file.

"What do you mean?" she asked without sitting up.

"Well, I'm an attractive, well-trained 22-year-old who can act, and I want to understand why I'm not getting called in to read more often."

"You're nice," she said as she pulled herself up, cigarette still burning between her lips.

"What do you mean?" I asked.

"You're nice-looking," she replied. "Don't call yourself attractive. You're not attractive. You're nice-looking. Here, let's look at your file."

She pulled out one of my headshots with what appeared to be seven or eight Post-it notes stuck on my face. This was my "file."

"Nice-looking, attractive...is there a difference?" I asked.

"Of course, there is! I don't send nice-looking people on auditions for attractive roles."

"Fine. Then why aren't I going out on more nice-looking auditions?"

"Oh, sweetheart, there aren't that many nice-looking roles."

People in Hollywood like to say shit like that all the time—shit that endows the speaker with being "in the know," while placing the subject clearly on the outside of that knowledge. I refused to participate.

"What do you mean?" I asked.

"You know what I mean," Patty quickly replied.

"No, I don't. That's why I asked. What do you mean?"

I didn't raise my voice, but clearly, I needed to become a Scientologist or something because I wasn't getting what this town was pushing.

"Randy, there are roles for attractive people, and there are roles for nice-looking people. Just like there are roles for black people and roles for white people. You don't expect me to send you out for a black-person role do you?"

I decided to ignore the ridiculous analogy and stay focused.

"I find it hard to believe there are so few nice-looking people roles." I paused to adjust my strategy.

"What about normal-looking people roles? Are there many normal-looking people roles?"

"You wanna go out for normal-looking people roles?"

I was stunned. I thought I was making a joke. I had no idea there was a "normal-looking" category.

"Sure, why not?" I said, thinking maybe I'd unlocked some secret door to success.

"You want to be identified as a normal-looking guy?"

"If there are more roles for normal-looking guys, YES!" I said entirely too loudly.

Patty pulled a Diet Coke from its plastic noose and placed it in front of me. I dug into my pockets and pulled out a cigarette. I was breathing the shit anyway. I might as well mainline it.

"Listen, until you start booking some work, your type is going to be a little fluid. Let's take a look at the auditions you've gone on." She scanned the curling yellow squares placed over my lips, eyes, and forehead. "How did the Subway sandwich commercial go?"

"They were looking for a skinny white guy to get sand kicked in his face by a couple of Mapplethorpe models."

"You too good to get a little sand kicked in your face?" she asked.

"No," I replied quickly.

"So what happened?"

"Aren't you my agent? Shouldn't you know this?"

"I can't know everything about all my clients, Randy. I'm only one person." I wasn't going to argue. She was only one person and, clearly, that was a problem for both of us. "So why do you suppose you didn't get the part?"

"They told me I was too skinny." I looked directly at her while I took a long drag off my cigarette. "They wanted someone with a little more meat on his bones."

"I remember that now."

"It's amazing what one person is capable of." Patty ignored my sarcasm.

"I remember because that was when I had the idea to send you out for the holocaust victim in that Nazi film." Patty seemed genuinely pleased with herself. She had not only read two yellow squares on my "face file," she had also managed to connect them.

"That's right," I said. "The naked Jew being hauled into the gas chamber."

"You're circumcised, right?" Patty asked.

"I am."

"So, what was the problem?" I allowed an uncomfortably long silence so the image of my liberated foreskin could linger with the smoke in the air.

"It turns out I'm too fat to be a dying concentration-camp victim."

"Oh, well. There you go."

Everything was so simple for Patty. She saw only black or white, never the vast spectrum of grays. She was an archetype.

Suddenly, it hit me. I was undefined: too skinny for sandwiches, too fat for the gas chambers, too ugly to be attractive, too attractive to be normal, and too fucking pale for Los Angeles. Of course! I needed to tap into my true identity.

What type of person was I? This deep metaphysical quandary spoke to the very core of my being. But this was Hollywood, and Hollywood doesn't give a shit about the core of anyone's being. My mind now in a full sprint, I could feel some terrible drama welling up inside of me.

"Why don't you do a little monologue?" Patty suggested delicately. She obviously noticed my rapidly shifting facial contortions, a trait that garnered me accolades from theater audiences and motion sickness from those who saw me on film.

"Right now?" I asked, being pulled from my profound personal explorations.

"Sure, why not? But make it funny. Last time, you depressed the GOD-DAMNED FUCKING SHIT out of me."

Whenever Patty cursed, she sounded like a 10-year-old performing a David Mamet monologue. Her emphasis on the dirty words made them seem awkward among the clean ones.

"I don't have..."

I realized that I was about to say the worst five-word sentence an actor can utter. "I don't have anything prepared" is "the dog ate my homework" excuse for the performer, immediately recognized as a cover for laziness.

"...time today," I finished with force and launched out of my chair. "I don't have time today." Patty seemed surprised by my abrupt declaration. "I have to get to work. But thanks for the talk. This has been really helpful."

"OK, then. We'll talk soon," she said, moving papers around her desk for no apparent reason. The conversation had an awkward beginning and an awkward conclusion, but somewhere in the middle was a diamond, smashed into existence by the immense pressure of all the bullshit.

As I walked out into the sun-baked parking lot, I sipped my Diet Coke and remembered too late I had already flicked my ashes in it. I immediately threw the can to the ground, sending soda flying across the pavement, and I headed toward my car. But, in the middle of the steaming hot asphalt, something stopped me. I was at a crossroads of some kind. Completely paralyzed, I literally didn't know which direction to walk. Hollywood may not care about the core of my being, but I did. My problem was that I didn't even recognize the core of my being. Was I nice-looking or normal-looking? What if I discovered I was attractive? Why is that important? And then I felt my core—or what I perceived to be my core—begin to rumble. It was talking to me.

Still unable to move, I focused my energy on my perceived core. A car drove onto the grass to get around me. Apparently, I was blocking the entrance to the parking lot, and my core didn't hear him honk.

Come on, core. Speak! Speak! Sweat broke out along my hairline. My nemesis, the afternoon sun, sprinkled cancer on my exposed scalp, where my hair had abandoned me. Another car entered the parking lot, and I considered moving to the side but decided against it. This watershed moment would not take place upstage right. These moments belong downstage center, fueled by the full power of the set from behind and the audience from the front. Here, the vast parking lot was my set, and the entering cars were now my audience.

My thoughts began accelerating due, no doubt, to the brilliant staging. What was my core saying? I need to be doing more theater! Yes! I quickly put that into my mental pocket. I have to find opportunities to express myself. OK, vague, but into the pocket. I don't want to be an attractive person. Wait, who doesn't want to be an attractive person? That's stupid. What a dumb thing to think. Don't call yourself dumb. That's not productive. Stay focused, Randy! What is my identity? Do I need an identity? Do you really want to sell sandwiches? I need a sandwich.

By now, my shirt stuck to my body, and sweat dripped off my nose. With cars lined up in front of me, four, maybe five deep, I was officially blocking traffic. Who were these people anyway? Why were they driving to this dive in the middle of the day? I tried to move my legs, but vertigo suddenly struck me. My core had something to tell me, and it wasn't going to let me go until I got the message. I could hear the cars honking. I looked up and saw Patty standing in the building's shade, alternately calling my name and taking a drag off her cigarette. Then, my core seized up, my eyes began to water, my cheek glands puckered and, as if I was sucker-punched, I doubled over and violently vomited in one continuous stream.

I stayed there for a moment, bent over, with bile dripping from my lips. The cars stopped honking. Everything had fallen silent. I gazed down at my sick, glistening in the sunlight. A long strand of spaghetti, just released by my throat, had fallen onto the pavement. Vomiting spaghetti feels terribly childish. I had to get out. I wasn't happy. My core had spoken, and I had to listen.

With tears clearing my eyes, I inhaled, stood up, and looked around. Sound returned. The motorists, now out of their cars, looked at me with concern but had not yet engaged. It was a drama after all, so the applause would be slow to come. A low-flying helicopter passed overhead. Patty walked back into the building, promising to return with water. I wiped my lips with my shirtsleeve. My future suddenly became clear. I had to get out of Los Angeles. I had to live the adventures I'd played out in my mind. I had to at least try and make my life everything I'd imagined it could be. I needed to begin again. And I needed to begin immediately. Every journey begins with the first step, right? Step one, step over the puke. Step two, move to New York. Step three, start living.

UNDER THE INFLUENCE

The enormity of the midtown towers had me transfixed. Jutting my head out the cab window, I looked to see if they stopped in any direction, but they didn't. It was an endless cavern of buildings, and I loved it. Light was coming from all directions, thanks to the spring fog and the freshly washed pavement. The cool moisture against my wine-warmed face invigorated me as if I were getting a high-speed tour through heaven. Earth slapped me in the face when I saw the cab's meter had just passed eight dollars.

"Excuse me. You can just let me out at the next corner," I said with as much authority as I could muster in my drunken state.

"You don't want to go to 78th?" the cabbie calls back in a thick Middle-Eastern accent.

"No. Just let me off here."

I scooted toward the right side door. You always exit a cab on the curbside, as I'd learned the hard way once when I barely escaped the wrath of a bicycle delivery man. I handed the cabbie my last 10-dollar bill and stepped out into the cool, misty night. I would have made it all the way home had I not insisted on that last glass of wine. But I had made it to 57th Street…in New York! It had only been two weeks since my friend Bobby and I made the 10-day trip across the country, but I already felt like a New Yorker.

I lit a cigarette and began strolling up First Avenue. Navigation is crucial in New York, as it's easy to get hypnotized by the endless energy around you. So I schooled myself quickly. In the Manhattan grid, north and south are the avenues. The street numbers get higher as you move north, smaller as you go south. East and west are the cross streets. And, as most crosstown streets are one way, once you know that traffic moves east on even-numbered streets and west on the odd numbers, your urban compass is complete.

Tonight, I had to walk due north 21 blocks, a little more than a mile. At 11 o'clock on a Tuesday evening, the East Side bars were crowded with recent college grads talking about their favorite subjects—money and marriage. At this moment in time, money outweighed marriage. This was May 1998. The country was enjoying a growth spurt like we'd never seen, and New York was bathing in money. Unfortunately, I wasn't. I had exactly $240 in my wallet and 100 times that amount in student loans and credit-card debt. One week out of work would have been devastating both to my diet and to my credit rating, which, as fucked up as it sounds, I prized more than my stomach. My timing couldn't have been better. In 1998, securing a job for a college graduate was as easy as showing up for the interview with a clean shirt and a good attitude.

The day after I arrived in New York, I reported to a temp agency for testing and placement. Within 24 hours, I was getting fingerprinted and pissing in a cup so I could report for work as a temporary assistant at Blah-Blah Big Bank. I found it odd they gave me a drug test to work at a bank. I thought all banker types were cocaine-snorting crooks. That's certainly the impression I got from the movies. But maybe that was just Hollywood or the '80s. Maybe bankers in the new millennium were going to be honest, drug-free citizens who would usher in a more responsible capitalism. Youthful idealism is an intoxicating tonic that can only be counteracted with a cynicism that grows like moss on the aged.

But I couldn't be concerned with whom I worked for or what I did. All I cared about was good pay, consistent hours, and the fact that, because it was a temp job, I could quit whenever I wanted. As it turned out, the consistency of a day job served as an invaluable anchor. New York is an overwhelmingly large place with an unlimited number of distractions for a 23-year-old. So, having a constant flow of cash to enjoy said distractions was important, as long as there was a commitment in the morning to prevent overindulgence. I wanted adventures, but I didn't want to get lost.

At first, the prospect of putting on a shirt and tie and reporting to "the man" gave me the willies. Scanning for stock footage was bad, but working at a bank sounded much worse, a whole new level of selling out. After a few short stints with some uninteresting people in some uninteresting cubicles, I began working with people I connected to more. That made all the difference.

"Randy, love!" Gabby would shout. "I can't read your writin'. What's this little snowman here?" More than half the people in this group were Caribbean, so the rhythm of the office conversation alone kept things interesting.

"That's an eight," I'd say to great laughter. Our area was so loud, you'd think it was a trading floor, but the difference was, we were laughing and joking, not screaming and shouting.

"Jesus, Randy," said my buddy Chris when he called me at work. "It always sounds like fucking happy hour over there."

"That's because it is," I said. "It is."

To this day, I truly believe you can be shoveling shit and not mind the smell, as long as you're in good company. The people in that group made working for "the man" a joy.

Finally, I arrived at the corner of First Avenue and 78th Street and plunged my key into the rusting metal door of my building. Bobby and I had sublet a one-bedroom apartment from a college friend who had moved to Queens with six months left on her lease. This gave us just enough time to find a more permanent abode. For the bargain price of $1,250 per month, we shared a 500-square-foot space on the fourth floor of a dilapidated walk-up building. As small as it was, it had all the character I wanted in a New York dwelling. The living room and bedroom each had a small window that looked out onto the brick wall of another building five feet away. The bathroom window, though, overlooked a small courtyard, across which you could see into the windows of a few dozen other apartments. And I discovered the wonderful world of voyeurism, a favorite New York pastime.

Reaching the fourth floor out of breath, I cursed the three cigarettes I inhaled on my walk from 57th Street and noticed the lights on in the apartment. I hadn't seen Bobby in several days. He didn't have a job yet, and he was getting lost on his adventures quite frequently. I opened the door and heard a conversation in the bathroom.

"Lobert! You have the debil in your eye! I see it! The debil is inside you." This, said in a thick Korean accent, was followed by an accent-free, "I love you so much. Why do you treat me like this? You're so smooth and wet. Can you stop being so wet? Of course, you can't. I keep turning you on."

Then, I heard the faucet switch on, a short burst of laughter, then tears, then laughter. The Korean accent continued. "Lobert! Stop it! You hurting me! Stop hurting me!" I considered leaving for a moment but glanced at the time and decided to engage.

I recognized the Korean voice instantly as a manifestation of his mother, a devout Christian who had an epic struggle with Bobby's homosexuality. It was hysterical to hear him imitate her in college, but what was happening in the bathroom wasn't imitation. This was possession. I closed the front door behind me and turned the lock. Across the living room, the bathroom door was open, and Bobby stood in his pajamas, talking directly to the sink.

"Bobby, are you OK? Who are you talking to?"

"I'm talking to... the sink," he replied.

"OK. Is everything OK?" I asked, very aware of his delicate state.

"No! Everything is *not* OK! I'm a fucking cokehead, OK? There is nothing OK with that!" And then he jumped back into the Korean accent. "It's the debil! Lobert is a junkie!"

Due to an undiagnosed allergy, Bobby couldn't drink, but he was prone to trying just about every other drug on the planet. For most people, this would be cause for concern, but Bobby's short attention span kept him from sticking to any one thing for long. This was both a blessing and a curse.

"OK," I said. "Wait, are you a cokehead or a junkie?"

"What do you mean?" Bobby said, looking up at me for the first time.

"Isn't a junkie a heroin addict? I mean, are you on coke or heroin?"

"Who gives a fuck what I'm called?" Bobby said adamantly. "I've been doing coke for four days straight! I'm a four-day-old crack-whore-bitch-ass."

Trying not to appear alarmed, I walked closer.

"Did you really have sex for crack or are you just being colorful?" I asked delicately.

"I'm being colorful. And it wasn't crack, it was coke! I'm a mess, I can't sleep, and I just want to go to sleep."

"I don't want to alarm you, but you might have some difficulty getting a job at a bank."

"What? Who the fuck cares!" he screamed. "I'm a cokehead, Randy. Don't you get it? I'm a COKEHEAD!"

"Yeah, I get it. I get it. Where did you get cocaine anyway?"

"I met this guy. We went to his house." The Korean accent jumped back in. "He's a homosexual. He has a da sex wit my boy." The fact that he was channeling his mother was creepy enough, but that she was now addressing me was over the top. He took a breath and continued in his own voice. "He was really hot. I went over to his house."

"So you did have sex for coke?" I asked.

"No. I had sex for sex. I did coke for coke. I hate myself." He returned his attention back to the sink. "Come back to Jebus. Jebus loves you. Stop being homosexual. No more coke with debil men. Come back to Jebus."

This was clearly going to be a very long night for Bobby and his mother.

"If you're gonna be up for a while, can you shut the door? I have to work in the morning," I said and began preparing for bed.

Without looking in my direction, he shut the door and, after several hours, I finally fell asleep to the sounds of a self-deprecating cokehead working out 20-some-odd years of issues with his mother.

That was the end of Bobby's coke days. He emerged from his bender largely unscathed. But every so often, when he went to the bathroom late at night, I would hear him curse at the sink. Like his mother, that smooth, wet menace would always haunt him.

I awoke the next morning and tumbled down the stairwell to push through another day. I'd already learned the most important lesson any new city dweller learns. New Yorkers work hard. This town is built on greed, power, and initiative, all of which take tremendous amounts of energy. I had fully subscribed to the adrenaline-fueled march toward...well, I guess it's called success.

The routine was the same every day. Up early. On the train. Coffee and a 30-second conversation with a man in a silver cart. Building pass, elevator, cubicle, phones, computers, paperwork, meetings, conference rooms, elevator, lunch sitting next to a fountain, reading news from a ticker, elevator, more work, elevator, street, done. This was the routine. Sleep, bathe, repeat.

I was quickly losing my lateral thinking skills, my "artistic sensibilities," if you will. I could feel my identity shifting to a different kind of person. And while I wouldn't mind being this person, it was not the person I truly wanted to be. That is not a subtle difference. Either I was tired or I identified with Bobby's desire for a change of direction, but the next day, something I saw moved me off the path toward a nice life and back on the path toward a full life.

After work, I headed down to the Village to meet some friends at a bar for beer and baseball. I didn't watch much baseball before moving to New York. But there's something about the teams and the fans in New York that makes it irresistible.

The subway moved slower than usual, and I preoccupied myself with how mad I was at the F train for making me late. Being mad at a late train is a futile exercise at which I excelled. New Yorkers alternate between Zen Buddhists and five-year-old brats when it comes to stalled or slow trains. On this particular day, I was a five-year-old. The train finally arrived at my station and I rushed to the exit. As I passed through the turnstile and headed up the stairs, I fell back from the putrid-sweet smell of stale pee on the platform. You smell a lot more pee in New York. You smell a lot more of everything in New York. I hurried to the surface and let the fresh air clean my nostrils.

Erasing the memory of the smell, I lit a cigarette and walked down Eighth Street. As I passed the window shoppers and summer students, I caught sight of a beggar. There wasn't anything particularly different about this beggar. Probably 10 years older than me, he was about my height and weight. His clothes were worn-looking, but they didn't appear soiled. He was holding out a wrinkled paper coffee cup trying to get the attention of each passerby. Something about him—his demeanor, his sincerity, maybe it was his humanity—had captured my imagination and compelled me to stop and watch.

He looked familiar to me somehow, and I continued to stare at him. I felt a little self-conscious for standing there gawking, but I couldn't help myself. The longer I observed, the more I realized nobody was making eye contact with him. Most people acted as if they hadn't seen him at all.

But they had.

And that was where the magic happened. I took note of everyone's reactions. Guilt and disgust were common. Sometimes, people would smile, not maliciously, but as if they were rejoicing in what they had. I saw relief, but I couldn't tell if it was relief they had made it past yet another beggar unscathed, or relief that *they* were not the ones begging. Everyone reacted. Even if their reaction was *not* to react, they had to expend some energy to do so. I watched them try to suppress their emotions. But the most fascinating aspect was that their reactions were never about the beggar but about themselves. Hate, fear, guilt, sorrow, pain, joy—all these emotions were sparked by the sight of the beggar, but the fuel was contained in the hearts of the viewers. And as they passed, they were changed. It was as if they walked into a cloud, only to emerge with white dust clinging to their hair, faces, and clothes, cloaking them in some new truth. Right then, I knew: I want to make theater that does that!

Looking for my own truth, I walked over and dropped five dollars into his cup.

"Thank you!" I said, imagining I was being cloaked in a beggar's fairy dust. I continued walking, peeking back, thinking he was some apparition that would magically disappear. But he didn't. He never disappeared. When I turned the corner, he was still there. Five innings and four beers later, I could still see him. That beggar was etched into my mind's eye, and that fairy dust was for real. His presence had clarified my desire. I wanted to create the beggar's effect. That was the kind of theater I wanted to do. That was the kind of impact I wanted my art to have. That was the kind of life I wanted to live.

NOT *THAT* KIND OF GAY

In less than two months, I landed my first New York acting gig. Scanning the trade papers for auditions, something I did once a week, I noticed a casting call for the touring production of a play called *Making Porn*. I had seen *Making Porn*, a very entertaining sex comedy about the gay porn industry, in Los Angeles. While the play focuses on beefy porn stars and a bounty of gratuitous nudity, the sympathetic boyfriend role didn't require hunkiness or nudity—a perfect part for me. Not that I'm shy about getting naked on stage, I'd done *Hair* in college. But there is a very big difference between hippie-naked and sexy-naked. Anyone can be hippie-naked, but sexy-naked requires countless hours in the gym and a kiss from the genetic gods.

After my audition, both the producer and the playwright immediately told me I was exactly what they were looking for. Two days later, at 7 a.m., my phone rang.

"Randy, it's Karen, the producer from the *Making Porn* audition."

"Hi, Karen! I wasn't expecting you to call so soon."

"Well, we really loved your audition and want to put you in the next show. We're working on a Boston run, but that's probably not going to happen for a while. In the meantime, we have a bit of an issue. Have you seen *Peepshow*?"

Although the auditions had taken place in the theater where *All Male Peepshow* was currently running, I didn't have 50 spare dollars for new shoes, let alone an off-Broadway play.

"No. I haven't seen it, but I'm sure it's good." I really *wasn't* sure, but it never hurts to suck up.

"Well, we have a cast member who is leaving, and we need someone to take his place pretty soon."

"How soon is pretty soon?"

"In three days," she responded with urgency and conviction. "We'll need you to come down and see the show tonight. Tomorrow, we'll put you backstage to shadow the actor you'll be replacing, and then you'll go on the next night. Can you memorize lines quickly?"

"Yeah, lines shouldn't be a problem. Three days. That's fast..."

"We'll pay you 200 dollars a week," Karen interrupted. "Stop by as soon as you can and pick up a script."

She wasn't going to take no for an answer. Of course, I could have said no. But it was an off-Broadway show—albeit a non-union show with producers that seemed a bit shady. But I could use the 200 bucks, and I really wanted to get on the boards. So, of course, I agreed and berated myself for even entertaining the idea of saying no.

"I have to go to work, but bring the script to the show, and I'll pick it up when I see you." I hung up and did a little victory dance on my bed. This move was paying off.

That night, Bobby and I met Karen in front of the subterranean Actors Playhouse on Seventh Avenue in the West Village. A heavyset woman in her mid-30s, Karen seemed nice but a bit pushy.

"Randy, glad you made it. Jonathan, take these programs to the booth. Let me get your script."

Leaving no space for me to talk, she kept barking orders to the cadre of young employees hovering all around her.

"Beth, can you run down to my house and get Randy his script? It's in a red binder on the dining-room table."

"I can pick it up after the show," I offered, taking my cue from the disgusted look on Beth's face.

"Don't worry, Beth will get it for you. Hurry up, Beth, I need you to take over the box office when you get back." And with that, Beth sped out into the West Village crowds. "Here are your tickets. Take notes. You'll be playing the role of Shane. Don't worry about learning everything. Concentrate on the entrances and the exits. You can make the part your own once we get you into the piece."

A shot of fear suddenly flew through my gut. I recognized the feeling immediately. A few years earlier, I was playing a plebeian in Shakespeare's *Julius Caesar*, and the Soothsayer's car broke down on his way back from Vegas. I had exactly one hour to learn the part...one miserable, torturous hour. Sure, it was only a few lines and hardly any stage business, but the very idea of forgetting something had me in a panic. Yes, it's "Beware the ides of March," one of the Bard's most recognizable lines. But fuck that up, even a little bit, and everyone will think you're an idiot. A misplaced breath could easily transform it into "Beware the hides of March."

Instead of relaxing and learning the role, I rattled through every possible mistake, convincing myself that my fate lay somewhere among the possible disasters. Luckily, the Soothsayer hitched a ride and arrived five minutes before curtain. Pushing this memory aside, I reminded myself this was *All Male Peep Show*, not *Hamlet*.

"Go sit down, and Beth will bring the script to you," Karen said.

Bobby and I descended into the small theater and found our seats. Beth appeared shortly, annoyed and out of breath.

"Thanks. You didn't have to run it over," I said, trying to comfort her. "It's not like I can read it during the show."

"I know," she replied with a snap, turning to leave.

"Um, excuse me, Beth," Bobby said. "Did we order this with a side of bitch?"

And he released a wicked laugh as the lights went down on the very stage I would be gracing in 48 hours.

Ninety minutes later, the lights came back up and we sat, dumbfounded, for a good minute. Finally, Bobby looked at me.

"Randy, I can't believe you're going to be in this show." I couldn't tell by his tone if he was excited or disgusted. "I mean, Randy, that show is… fleshy. I might need to go home and masturbate right now!"

"Yeah," I replied with a sigh. "It's pretty fleshy all right."

The next night, fighting the "*hides* of March" fears, I reported to the theater to shadow the departing actor. I arrived two full hours before curtain and began my warm-ups. Since I wasn't performing that night, the warm-up was unnecessary, but I wanted to set up a routine to help me maintain focus.

The other actors started wandering in, and they all looked at me as if I were some exotic animal performing an elaborate mating ritual. It took a while before I realized their odd glances weren't because I was a new addition to the backstage family but because I was warming up. Karen had taken to calling me the "real actor," and, flattery aside, I wasn't sure what she meant until this moment. Most of the performers—good-looking, hard-bodied model types—had little or no acting training. A few of them, I would find out later, actually made their living as male escorts. This was not the warm-up crowd. This was the fluffing crowd. I was completely out of my element. If I was going to share the stage with models, I had to bring something else to the table. Good acting, it seemed, would be my only option.

A half-hour before the show, the star walked backstage, noticed me right away, and came over to introduce himself.

"You must be the new guy," he said, extending his hand toward me. "I'm Jeff Stryker."

His hair was perfect. His bronzed face exhibited excellent proportions, and his handshake was confident and firm.

"Randy Anderson. Nice to meet you."

Jeff Stryker was a movie star. I had heard of him, but aside from last night's show, I'd never seen any of his work, something I would not disclose to any of my cast mates. I needed to fit in.

"Welcome to the show. Have you met everyone yet?"

I was taken aback by his charm and friendliness. And his eyes were so...sympathetic. I found this odd because he's famous for his prison videos, and sympathetic eyes are not what you'd expect from someone sodomizing an inmate.

"No," I replied. "You're actually the first person I've met. I've been warming up."

"You mean, like yoga?"

"Well, yes. Kind of. Just getting my instrument warmed up."

"Oh, I get it! Cool. I don't get my instrument warmed up until the second act," he said, laughing at his own joke. "Come on. I'll introduce you to the rest of the cast."

He took me around and introduced me to everyone. I'm not shy and had no trouble saying hello to my cast mates. But the conversations quickly became labored. These fellas lived in "gay land," and I was clearly a tourist. I was, and still am, a terrible dresser. Show tunes aren't my thing. Fire Island sounds to me like another name for hell. I just didn't get half of what they were saying.

"Are you a friend of Dorothy?" they'd ask. Sure, I was a friend of Dorothy. She was our receptionist at the bank. The deeper we got into it, the more foolish I felt. It was as if they spoke a different language. I'm just not that kind of gay. I'm a guy who sleeps with guys.

The next night, I made my debut. It's doubtful I was any good, but I hit all my marks and said all my lines, and even if I didn't, nobody noticed. I settled into the show though, and by the end of the first week, I seized ownership of the role.

Each night, after the curtain fell, the cast would descend on a restaurant followed by an all-night excursion to a trendy Chelsea nightclub. Due to a severe lack of funds, I never participated in these ritualistic post-show outings. Instead, I would munch on a homemade peanut-butter-and-jelly sandwich as I walked the 70 blocks back to my apartment. The next night, in the dressing room, I would hear stories of drug-induced dance marathons and torrid sexual escapades with good-looking strangers. Even if I had the money, I'm pretty sure I wouldn't fit in, but the fact I was financially barred from this world filled me with envy.

All that changed with a very special invitation.

One of Jeff's celebrity fans had arranged for the cast to occupy the VIP room with "everything taken care of" at a sizzling hot nightclub on the West Side. This would be my chance to peek into, if not fully participate in, this other world.

After the show, we ran into the dressing room and got out of our costumes, which for several actors just meant slipping out of their thong underwear. Nice pants and loosely buttoned shirts flew onto chiseled bodies, and the air quickly filled with hairspray and heavy cologne. A marijuana pipe began floating around the room. I took a few puffs, and Jeff poked his head in.

"Guys, the limo is here. Let's go!"

Limo! I hadn't heard about a limo. I could barely contain my excitement. Apparently, when someone says, "everything is taken care of," they mean they're sending a limo. I finished combing my hair as fast as I could. I had never been in a limousine in my life. Despite my measly 200-dollar-a-week salary and the decrepit state of this theater, I felt I had arrived. I was being picked up in a limousine and taken to the VIP room of an exclusive club.

I hit the sidewalk as everyone was piling into the car. Jeff brazenly took a puff from his pipe on the street and handed it to me at hip height. I took a drag, exhaling the smoke into the warm summer air while absorbing the bustling nightlife around me.

"This is great, isn't it?" Jeff said, as his beautiful lips curled up, part Cheshire cat, part schoolboy.

"Thank you for sharing this," I replied. "This is a real treat for me."

"My pleasure," he said, placing his hand on my shoulder. "I'm glad you're finally coming out."

Just then, the limo driver called Jeff over to the passenger-side window. I stood on the sidewalk and lit a cigarette. The city still felt new to me, and I loved letting the energy play off my senses. Jeff stepped back from the window. His mood had changed dramatically.

"This sucks," he said.

"What? What sucks? What's going on?" I asked in rapid succession.

"The driver says we can't go with this many people. He was told he'd be picking up eight people, and we've got 12."

"Well, how many people can fit in the car?" I asked.

He was Jeff Stryker after all. He must know something about limousines.

"I don't know. He just said he's only taking eight. That's what he was told, and that's what he's doing. People are going to have to get out."

I quickly calculated. With 10 people in the car now, Jeff and I made it 12. So four people would have to be left out. There was no way I'd be getting in.

"Hold on a second," I said with certainty. "I'll take care of this."

This was my first limo ride. I was not about to be left behind. I don't know if it was the pot or the city, but suddenly I became the very person I'd always imagined: a confident, fast-talking New Yorker.

I knocked on the passenger-side window with the middle knuckle of my middle finger, something I'd never done before. The driver looked over and lowered the window. I opened the door, sat down, and closed it behind me. I was going to have a private conversation with this man face-to-face, like a mobster.

"Look, I can't take you all," he said.

"What's your name?" I asked, hoping to get personal.

"I can only take eight people," he replied, obviously not wanting to divulge his name.

"I'm Randy. What's your name?"

"Paul."

"OK, Paul. Why can't you take 12 people?"

"I was told to pick up eight people. And that's all I can take." Paul was determined to follow orders. I noticed a plaque on the dashboard that read "maximum occupancy 10 people."

"Well, it says there you can take 10 people," I said barely recognizing myself. Where did this attitude come from?

"Yeah, the car can take 10 people, but I was told to pick up eight."

"But, technically, you can take 10, right?"

"Yes."

"Great!" I was making progress and my knees pulled further apart as I settled into the leather seat. "So, listen, we're a cast of 12 people, and we'd really like to go to this party together. It's only a few miles. Can you please make an exception? Nobody is going to know."

"Fine. I'll take 10, but legally I can't take any more than that," Paul said with finality.

"Do you watch porn, Paul?" He looked at me with confusion. "Because right out there is quite possibly the most famous porn star in the world.

"That's a guy," Paul shouted.

"Well, you need guys in porn, too!" I exclaimed, knowing now Paul was straight.

"I thought Ron Jeremy was the most famous porn guy," Paul replied with only moderate certainty.

"Great. So, you do watch porn. Who doesn't, right? Anyway, that man there is Jeff Stryker, arguably the most famous male porn star in the world. And much better-looking than Ron Jeremy, wouldn't you agree?"

"He's all right."

I knew I was wearing Paul down with the porn talk and decided to bring it home.

"Did you know that his dildo is the best-selling dildo in the world? More women, and men for that matter, are getting off solo with a model of that man's dick. Pretty cool, wouldn't you say?"

"No," Paul stated simply.

I had gone too far, and it was time to wrap this up. Snapping my knees together and sitting forward, I locked eyes with Paul.

"Listen, this is supposed to be a really fun night for us. We just want to get to the party. If you could squeeze one more person in the back, I'll ride up here with you."

Paul thought about this for a moment and, afraid I'd start talking about porn again, he agreed.

"But you have to ride up here," he reiterated.

"Not a problem. Thank you," I said, as I exited the car.

"What happened?" asked Jeff, anxiously. "What did he say? Can we go?"

"Get in the car. He'll take us all."

I saw Jeff's eyes leap with excitement. And I watched them carefully as they came back down to meet mine.

"Man, you're so cool," he said as he kissed me on the lips, which made me feel good and weird and sexy. Jeff isn't gay, but folks in the sex business are a tactile bunch. I stood there on the sidewalk and savored the tingle.

"Be careful," he continued as he walked to the back door. "The one-eyed snake will be gunning for you on closing night!"

And with a wicked grin, he jumped into the back of the limousine. I smiled at a stranger passing by and took my place in the front seat next to Paul, who would dominate the conversation with sports. Together, we drove "those gays" to the ball.

Once at the club, I learned pretty quickly my PB&J walks provided a far more satisfying post-show experience. The club was crowded, the private room was loud, and my cast mates spent most of their time running around looking for hookups. So, I settled on the couch and listened to Jeff's stories about his life in Hollywood.

Closing night came sooner than I expected. While I had only been doing the show for a month, my cast mates had been at it for almost six, and they all seemed eager to move on. I'd miss the money and I'd miss Jeff, but that was about all. This wasn't my kind of theater. I needed more brain and less body. I was still thinking about that beggar and how I wanted to make theater that would create a deeper impression. But, boy, was I going to miss that 200 bucks every week. This dominated my thoughts as I moved through our final performance.

As the last scene approached, Jeff came up to me backstage and whispered into my ear, "You've got 10 minutes. Ten."

I didn't know what that meant, but I knew it couldn't be good. Jeff had wanted to deflower me on stage in some way since I joined the show.

The lights shift, and I take my place on the stool next to my fellow actors. This scene takes place at a male strip club, and we're the eager patrons, a sort of "on-stage audience." The music gets louder, and Jeff appears center stage in a white toga. The audience bursts into applause. Jeff walks a few steps forward and rips off his toga in one quick and seamless motion. The audience resumes their applause, which quickly deteriorates. Some people need their hands to cover their eyes; others, to stop their mouths from making an audible gasp; and others still simply throw them up into the air.

Jeff is naked. That comes as no surprise. That was what they paid for. What nobody expects to see is Jeff's fully erect penis. You don't become a world-famous porn star with seven inches. Jeff has an impressive organ. Even the cheap seats have a great view.

Jeff pauses through the initial surprise because he knows they'll settle into more applause, and it's up to us on stage to give them their cue. We start clapping and shouting. The real audience follows suit. Jeff slowly removes the rubber band–like cock ring encircling the base of his member and shoots it into the audience. It flies into the seventh row, followed by a comet-like spray of body oil.

Jeff prances around the stage, shaking every bit of what God gave him, and then he turns to us. Usually, he would start downstage left, shake a little for the actor downstage from me, and then breeze past me putting a finger on my chin. It was a sweet gesture he had incorporated in after my first few days with the show. And, despite the fact he was erect and glistening head to toe with baby oil, I would still find it charming.

However, this time he doesn't wander down left. He walks purposefully upstage toward me. Fast. I have no idea what his plan is, but from the shouts around me, I could tell the other actors do. He stops two feet in front of me. A safe distance, I think, as he puts his hand on top of my head. My instinct is to lean back, but he's putting too much pressure on my head.

Suddenly, I realize we're in an improv moment. The first rule of improv is to always say "yes." When someone offers a situation, you accept it. Then, there is the "and," which is where you add to the situation. Yes. And. Accept the situation, and add to it. This is the golden rule, but can that really apply to onstage fellatio? I mean, even if I wanted to, I'm not sure I'd be able to. And if I did, what would my "and" be? Yes, I'll accept your cock into my mouth. And...I'm going to tickle your balls? Woefully few options appeared acceptable to my palate.

After a couple of lewd hip gestures, Jeff releases my head and turns around. That is it. That is all they had planned. I begin to laugh in relief, and the guys around me point and laugh. That is it, an innocent joke. A mock blowjob gesture. The actor behind me gives me the "gotcha" push on my shoulder, and I collapse forward in laughter just as Jeff begins to twirl.

As I'm sitting up, I see it coming. Jeff is in a fast twirl, and as any twirling 10-year-old will tell you, twirlers tend to wander. I have just enough time to close my eyes before I hear the loud clap of flesh-on-flesh. His penis slaps me right on my left cheek. Luckily, he has softened up a bit during the dance so it's more like being hit by a water balloon than a frozen sausage. I look up to see Jeff react in horror as I bring my hand to my now oily face. Clearly, he didn't intend to dick-slap me, but there we are, on stage in front of 200 people.

Wiping the oil from my face, I assess the situation. Aside from the slapping noise, it appears the audience didn't notice the beating. We all resume our actions, and the show proceeds as usual. As the final curtain falls, I rehearse an explanation for the black eye I imagine forming on my face.

Backstage, Jeff found me nursing my reddened cheek. "Randy, I'm so sorry. I didn't see you."

"Don't worry about it," I said, smiling. "It was an accident."

"Some accident too!" Jeff said, laughing. "But, really, I'm sorry. Are you OK?"

"I'm fine. I just didn't expect to get bitten by the one-eyed snake." And Jeff kissed my cheek.

"You're a sweet man," he said.

I watched him walk away and thought about how fond I'd grown of him and how I was going to miss seeing him every day. I kept staring as he placed himself, in his bathrobe, at the exit of the theater so he could shake the hand of every departing audience member. I watched for a few minutes. Some people refused to take his hand. They'd seen him grab his penis with that hand.

Touching my face, I smiled. I had developed a little crush on this porn star. And it had nothing to do with his chiseled torso and magnificent penis. No, I'm not that kind of gay. I liked his eyes.

.

WE'RE ALL IMMIGRANTS

After its skyscrapers, New York City is probably best known for its immigrants. Being a major point of entry for people from all over the world gives New York its unique diversity. People come here in search of a better life. Some find it. Others do not. But the people who come here have a dream, a vision of the life they'd like to call reality. I don't mean just international immigrants. U.S. citizens also immigrate to this city in search of a better life. That's certainly what brought me here. I had a vision for how my life was going to be, and day-by-day I was making that a reality.

When our sublet expired, Bobby and I found a large two-bedroom apartment on 109th Street and Columbus Avenue. It had a giant living room, two ample bedrooms, and 10 windows on three exposures. Easily three times the size of our Upper East Side place, this new apartment provided lots of room to shelter future immigrants—our friends, who were lining up to take a crack at the Big Apple.

Stephanie arrived first. Having recently graduated from our alma mater, she came to pursue a singing career. The day of her arrival, Bobby and I met her at the Port Authority bus station. We were certain Stephanie, a magnificent actress and a talented singer/songwriter, would adapt to the city in a New York minute. Standing among the crowds, we saw her bounce into the station with her bleached-blond hair framing her ear-to-ear smile. She was so excited to be in New York that when she waved to us, she dropped one of her bags and hit the person next to her on the head.

"Oops, sorry!" she said as she laughed.

"Damn, girl," Bobby said under his breath. "This is going to take some work."

Perhaps it would take her an L.A. minute. We walked over to help with her bags. Boy, did she have an aura around her. Was it peppiness? Maybe cheerfulness? Then, I recognized it. It was happiness. I'm not saying New Yorkers aren't happy. I hadn't stopped being happy since I got here. We just don't wear our happiness on our heads like big summer hats.

"Girl, we've got to tone you down!" Bobby said as he embraced her.

"What's wrong?" Stephanie asked, slapping his back. "I'm happy to be here."

"This is New York, honey. Nobody cares. Keep your happiness hidden, or somebody's gonna steal it." And he let out an infectious laugh as we walked out of the station scanning the crowd for potential happiness-snatchers.

Stephanie settled into our apartment, where she'd live until she found her own place. But with the extra money she paid us, we secretly hoped she'd stay for a while. Our own need for money was turning us into sofa slumlords.

Bobby helped her get a temp job in his office at the World Trade Center. Once he flushed the cocaine from his system, he had buckled down and found a respectable job—a job he truly hated. So, he was glad to bring in a familiar face.

I was glad for him, too. A week before, he had thrown himself against his 67th floor window in an attempt to "escape it all." His 140-pound body, no match for the industrial-strength windows, bounced right off. After multiple attempts, he resigned himself to finish his work, clock out, and live another day. Maybe Stephanie could share some of her happiness with him and keep him from smudging any more windows.

Stephanie attacked the city with an absolute fearlessness. She met people left and right and went to every audition she could find. One afternoon, she joined me on an audition for a European tour of *Hair*. They were looking for male tribe members, specifically for Berger, a role I'd played in college. Confident with the music, I thought I'd give it a shot.

"I'm just going to tag along like a little sister!" said Stephanie, bouncing around me.

"They're not seeing girls you know," I said, as we took the elevator up to the midtown studios.

"I know," she replied. "I want to meet James Rado." He was one of the play's authors.

"I highly doubt James Rado will be there, but you never know."

He wouldn't be there. Casting directors, not authors, run auditions like these. The directors aren't even there, for that matter.

We got to the reception area and saw about 20 cookie-cutter hippy dudes, all with scraggly long hair and chiseled jowls.

"Well, at least you'll stand out," said Stephanie, referring to my clean-cut banker hair parted to the side and my button-up shirt tucked neatly into my pleated pants. "Here, change into this." She handed me a bag.

"What's this?" I asked.

"Just go change," she ordered. "I'll sign you in."

"You brought me a change of clothes?"

"Yes! Bobby and I pulled these out of your closet last night. Now, go change."

I looked in the bag and saw the patched jeans I had worn in our college production.

"I can't believe you brought these." My fashion failures are legendary among those who know me.

"We knew you'd show up to the audition looking too preppy! Now, go change. You've got to warm up."

In her instantaneous transformation from little sister to stage mom, Stephanie pushed me toward the bathroom. By the time my hippie-self emerged, she had befriended all the other hippie dudes. Being the only girl in the lobby made her quite popular.

"Yeah! You look so much better," Stephanie shouted across the lobby. "That's my best friend. Don't those jeans look great?"

Mildly embarrassed, I found a corner and quietly warmed up my voice.

When they called my name, I headed toward the audition room, realizing that, despite the hippie pants, I still looked too preppy for this part. This show occupied a different time in my life, and I started to question why I was even there. But there I was, so I might as well sing them a song. I walked into the room to find a long table filled with a bunch of kids around my age and one very hippie man, who looked to be in his 60s, sitting right in the middle.

"Hi, Randy," he said, looking down at my headshot. "I'm James Rado, and these are some members of the tribe that will be going on tour with us. Nice pants! Hey, Joanne, look at his pants! They're far out!"

"Thanks," I said, stunned to be in the presence of the writer. Big brother know-it-all doesn't know it all after all. "They belonged to one of my college professors. He wore them when he ushered for the production in San Francisco back in the '70s."

"Way back then, huh? That's far out! I dig it." He was so incredibly hippie. "What are you going to sing for us today?"

I paused, mentally thanking my friends for packing the jeans, and then sang the show's title song. When I finished, James thanked me. We talked a bit about the show and how it had woven itself into the fabric of my life. He countered that the show continued to *be* his life. Then, I remembered a question I had when I first did the show.

"James, when you were writing *Hair*, did you feel like you were writing something special?"

I've always been fascinated with the levels of artistic self-awareness. He paused, and looked me dead in the eye.

"Yes, of course. We all did. Why would you ever want to do something you didn't feel was special?"

I realized instantly I already knew that answer. Anyone who's seen a therapist for five minutes knew that answer. But that really wasn't the way I'd intended the question to be heard, which actually gave me some insight into this man's self-image. And suddenly, in my mind, the conversation turned into a kind of verbal Rorschach test, which is dangerous when dealing with a 60-something hippie, so I thanked him and walked out the door. The second I entered the reception area, I locked eyes with Stephanie and mouthed the name *James Rado*. She jumped up and bolted past me into the studio.

"Hi, Mr. Rado. My name is Stephanie," I heard her say as she entered the room. "I know you're not seeing women..." I intentionally got in the monitor's way and let the door close.

"She's a friend of James," I lied, as I headed for the bathroom to peel the jeans from my legs. A full 20 minutes later, Stephanie emerged, beaming with excitement. They'd had quite a conversation, and he even had her sing a song. It was a magical afternoon for both of us.

We spent the rest of the day skipping through the caverns of midtown, singing our favorite songs from the show, and talking about our dreams. Stephanie, intent on getting a record deal, wanted to record an album so badly she could taste it.

I was less focused. I knew I wanted to make theater. But in what capacity? I'm an actor, yes. But so far, the auditioning thing, while mildly productive, wasn't nourishing me. And the shows I was auditioning for were, well... they didn't feel special. Something was still missing.

In our wandering, we happened across a building that housed a recording studio. Stephanie, seeing it as a sign, decided she needed to take the elevator up to the front desk and ask for a job. She didn't come back down for an hour. While I waited on the street, drinking coffee and chain-smoking, she was up on the 29th floor flirting with some rapper/engineer dude.

They didn't have any jobs for her at the moment, but the rapper/engineer had a home studio up in the Bronx. They instantly started dating and, a week later, Stephanie moved in with him to lay down her record. Now that's focus.

My focus wasn't coming as quickly. But I too had started seeing someone, someone who would be my first significant relationship. I'd dated a little in L.A. and had a few flings in New York, but nothing meaningful ever materialized.

C.J., as everyone called him, was a handsome, fair-haired guy my age. An aspiring writer, he worked for an Internet company. In the late '90s, everyone seemed to be working for an Internet company. With ridiculous amounts of money being thrown at start-ups left and right, C.J. figured he just needed to put in his 12 years and he'd be ready to retire at 35. It seems laughable in retrospect, but to a 23-year-old at the turn of the 20th century, this appeared fully achievable, a goal shared by many bright-eyed youths.

I didn't have any designs on retiring young. I hadn't even really started my career yet. Besides, I firmly believed that retirement was a post-war concept designed to keep the worker bees happy. To me, it was the dangling carrot that justified doing something you didn't really like instead of following your bliss and living in the present. Ironically, my job at Blah-Blah Big Bank was to package and sell 401(k) plans to mid-sized companies.

"So, she just moved out?" C.J. asked me after I had told him about Stephanie's departure.

"Just like that. She said something about not being comfortable at our place," I said, getting comfortable in his bed.

"This guy is practically a stranger. She's going to be more comfortable there?"

"So she says. And I guess this guy is some kind of rapper, or he runs in those circles. I don't know. It all sounds kind of fucked-up, but she really wants to make an album. I think she'll do just about anything to make that happen."

I pondered the dedication she possessed, which made me question my own drive. C.J. must have picked up on this.

"Would you do anything to act?" he asked me, propping his head on his hand and looking down at me.

"I don't think so. Obviously, not anything. But..." I paused, because the conversation was getting scary, but I pressed on. "I don't know if that's what I want to do. I don't know. I'm confused."

"If I asked you right now, what you want to be when you grow up, what would you say?" C.J. asked, playfully jumping on top of me.

"Right now?"

"Right now!" he said, pinning my shoulders to the mattress.

"Happy."

"I love you."

"I love you too," I replied.

Happy. That was a total cop-out answer if ever I'd uttered one, better suited for a soap opera than...wait...did we just say we *loved* each other? Suddenly, I felt crazier than Stephanie. Sure, she may have moved in with some dude she'd only known for a week, but surely she didn't *love* him. I knew she had at least that much sense. What was happening to me? This was the first time I'd ever uttered such a thing. It felt good...and scary...and good...and dangerous...but so good.

Our 109th Street vacancy was next filled a few weeks later when Big Rob made his journey east. At six-foot-six and a solid 250 pounds, Big Rob is a loud, gentle, offensive, and charming teddy bear. Unlike the rest of us, who came to New York to chase our dreams, Big Rob was here to sow some wild oats. His grandmother had recently passed, and he had decided to use some of his inheritance on a year or two fucking around in New York City. He just wanted to check it out, have some adventures, and hang with his friends.

Shortly after his arrival, he celebrated his 30th birthday. To most of us, who were five or six years younger than him, turning 30 seemed like a very big deal. We really wanted to mark the occasion. And what better way to do that than to take the birthday boy to Lucky Cheng's?

Big Rob had a thing for Asian women, and Lucky Cheng's was New York's premier Asian restaurant and karaoke bar. Actually, it's New York's premier *drag* Asian restaurant and karaoke bar. Sure, some of the waitresses aren't exactly girls, and those that *are* girls weren't exactly born that way. But they are all beautiful, so we figured he wouldn't care.

During the dinner show, Big Rob enjoyed a lap dance, multiple crotch grabs, and a humiliating stage stunt involving whipped cream and a banana. This restaurant was tailor-made for an uncensored kind of guy like Big Rob. It wasn't until we retired to the downstairs karaoke bar that the magic of the evening really took hold of him.

While in the middle of my signature karaoke song, *Puff the Magic Dragon*, I noticed a very tall woman—arguably, the prettiest one in the whole place—sitting on Big Rob's lap. I recognized her immediately as the hostess that had Big Rob do all those stage stunts. She was now enjoying a drink with, or should I say, *on* the birthday boy. She had Big Rob in a trance. Just as I threw myself into the most dramatic and tragic part of the song, *"One great aye did happen, Jackie Paper came no more,"* I saw them lock their open mouths in a passionate exploration of dental hygiene. It wasn't a romantic kiss. It was a sexual kiss, charged with a thousand volts of lust and curiosity. And before I could sing the final chorus, they were running out of the bar.

We didn't see or hear from Big Rob for three days. He had been abducted by a six-foot Japanese transsexual waitress. We didn't see that coming and weren't sure what to do. I tried to find him, but a restaurant visit proved useless. There seemed to be some sort of Asian tranny mafia that protected the privacy of its members. They wouldn't even tell me her name or if she had come to work lately. The more I searched, the more I imagined him trapped in some dungeon somewhere, enslaved by angry Asian-Amazonian transsexuals.

When Big Rob finally *did* come home, Bobby, C.J., and I attacked him with questions and angry instructions about how he needed to check in with us once in a while.

"What have you been doing?" I screamed. Do you know how worried we've been? New York is a dangerous place."

"Who *was* that woman?" Bobby followed.

"Was she a woman, or was he a man?" C.J. asked in his perfect grammar. Big Rob barely listened to our words, let alone our grammar. He just walked past us, exhausted from days and days of God-knows-what.

"Her name is Megumi. She's so sophisticated and poised. She has this wild laugh. And she's got this really pronounced jaw, I guess because she used to be a man, but when she laughs it moves up and down. It's like that Asian guy who always wins the hot dog–eating contest at Coney Island. You know who I'm talking about? The little guy. You know how his jaw goes up and down real fast as he pushes the hot dog down his throat? That's what it's like when she laughs."

We stood there in silence. It was quite a visual. He then stripped down to his baggy white Fruit of the Looms and plopped down on the couch. "That was the best birthday present ever!"

Poor guy didn't know it yet, but it would be months before he heard from Megumi again. Their three-day love fest resulted in a month-long hospital visit for vaginal reconstruction surgery. No matter how advanced we think we are, mankind still can't make them as well as Mother Nature does.

All was right with the world. Big Rob was free from the shackles of a medically constructed vagina. Stephanie was laying tracks with her rapper/engineer boyfriend in the Bronx. Bobby was actually sleeping now. And C.J. and I were curled up in my tiny twin bed slowly drifting to sleep. And even though I was still searching for my focus, sleep came easy. Sleep always comes easily when you're keenly aware of your youth—when your dreams, if not your whole life, lie ahead of you.

Part II
THE BEGGARS GROUP

EAST FOURTH STREET

My first New York autumn introduced itself so subtly, it was mid-November before I realized we were best friends. Fall has always felt like a time for new beginnings. Because of the scholastic calendar, I associate the falling leaves with new challenges and opportunities. And, even though I've been out of school for years, I still get excited about the potential of something new happening as the season changes. That must have been in the air that crisp fall day when my buddy Chris and I settled into Swifts, a small East Village bar, to drink a few pints.

"I think people want to be challenged," I said. "This is a time of great prosperity, and Broadway is able to take more chances."

"What chances?" Chris asked. "Broadway doesn't take chances."

"Sure, every time you produce a show, you're taking a chance," I replied. "It's risky, that's a given, but there's a big difference between doing *Guys and Dolls* and *Beauty Queen of Leenane*. People are happy now. When people are happy, they're willing to challenge themselves when they go to the theater. They want to explore the depths of the human experience. When times are hard, people want to escape into something easily digestible because they're experiencing the depths of human experience on a daily basis. It's a way of balancing ourselves. This is 1998. By and large, Americans lives are awesome. So, it's Broadway's turn to do the exploring."

Chris looked unconvinced as he took a sip of his beer. "So, what kind of theater are you doing? How would you classify *Peep Show*?"

"I wouldn't call *Peep Show* easily digestible, if that's what you mean, but it was definitely fluff," I replied.

"Fluffer theater!" he said, ribbing me on my New York debut. "But seriously, what are you doing next?"

"I'm not sure. I've been a little lost lately. I'm not getting into the whole audition scene. I *have* started writing a play, though."

"Oh, yeah? What about?"

Now, I have a habit, at times, to talk endlessly about my latest project. It's over-enthusiasm, I guess, but it usually bores the listener. So, when I'm discussing a new project, I like to break it down into three segments: the title, the tag line, and the description. Since everyone wants the title and the tag line, I give that first. And then, if there's still interest, I give the full description, which, if done right, invites a good discussion.

"It's called *Testing Average*." Title.

"It's an exploration of our society's 'not-so-subtle' caste system." My working tag line.

Chris still appeared interested, so I proceeded to the description. "It follows the life of a smart young man working his way through our society's prescribed steps toward success: from honor roll to SATs to Ivy League to a good corporate job to a wife, some kids, and a house. But..."

"There's always a but," Chris interjected.

"...the untimely death of his mentally disabled brother derails his plan and sends him on a quest to redefine the meaning of success."

Chris paused for a moment.

"Wow, that sounds great," he said. "And how does he redefine success?"

"That's the big question, isn't it? And truth be told, I don't know yet. It's tricky because I keep getting hung up on the defining bit. According to the dictionary, success is the prosperous termination of endeavors. If you define success for yourself—money, fame, physical strength, whatever—you should be able to achieve it, like a goal. This is what I believe success looks like, and this is what I'm going to do to achieve it. But I'm not interested in defining temporary success. I'm interested in defining a successful life. And shit happens in our lives that forces us to change our definition of success constantly. And if that's the case, success should be a fluid concept, and if we go with the fluidity, then a successful life is the journey as opposed to the task accomplished. It's not point B. It's the line between point

A and B. It's the looking back from your deathbed and feeling good about the journey, not necessarily the accomplishments. That's part of it, too. But it's not everything. And I think that, in our society, we put too much emphasis on the accomplishments and not enough on the journey. Why else do Americans take a quarter of the vacation time all the other industrialized nations do? 'Cause we gotta get shit done. And we're gonna spend 95 percent of our lives getting shit done and 5 percent of our lives living."

I took a sip of beer. It was the only way to shut myself up.

"That's some heavy shit."

"I know. Confucius heavy. And in that spirit, the point is not to know the answers but to ask the questions and contemplate. Because once you think you've arrived at the answer, the question has already changed, which is really what the play is going to end up asking you to do. Contemplate, I mean. It will be a contemplative play."

"Well, when are we going to see it?" he asked, as if I already had a plan.

"Ha!" I laughed. "When I finish writing it and someone decides to produce it."

"Why don't you just produce it yourself?" he suggested simply, as he sipped his beer and checked out a girl on her way to the bathroom. For Chris, New York was a savanna, and he was always on safari.

"Could you imagine?" I replied softly, ready to move on with the conversation.

"Why not?"

"I don't have any money," I said, as if he should know. "That's why not."

"You don't need that much money. You'd be surprised. I'm not saying it'll be cheap, but you won't lose your shirt. You'll still be able to eat. You know what I mean? You should look into it."

Chris was in full scout mode now. He'd traced the origin of the bathroom-bound coed and discovered a whole flock of girls at a table by the door.

"How much does it cost to rent a theater?" I asked him.

"We rented this space called the Red Room last month. That was really cheap. It's right down the street, above the KGB bar. You should talk to them. I bet they'd work with you. Hold the fort. I'll be right back."

Chris grabbed his beer and moved into the flock of girls he'd been eyeing. He was a flirt, not a slut, so I knew he'd return, glowing with girl giggles, and we could finish our conversation.

I went up to the bar to order another beer. Could I really produce the play myself? The thought filled me with an excitement I hadn't felt in years. This play felt special to me, and regardless of what direction my career was going, I truly wanted to work on something that felt special. Before the bartender could take my order, I grabbed my jacket and headed toward the door. I passed Chris, who was already deep in conversation with the ladies.

"I'm going to see a man about a theater," I said, opening the door. "I'll be right back."

"Cool, man! I'll be here."

And the sounds of the bustling bar turned to an expansive, quiet cold. The low autumn light cast a magical hue on the buildings. I took a deep breath and smiled at the smell of crisp air and the visual stimulation. The East Village is the picture of downtown cool. Aisles of tenement houses, adorned with fire escapes frame the sky. Funky bars, boutique shops, and performance spaces decorate the street level. Looking west, I see hordes of NYU students darting through the streets. I cross Bowery and look up toward Astor Place, with its rotating black square sculpture propped up on one corner. If you get a few people around it, you can make that thing spin pretty fast, which was a popular 3 a.m. activity on a Saturday night.

My gaze shot forward as I continued down East Fourth Street. This block, between Bowery and Second Avenue, already held so many memories for me. Even before I moved to New York, my short visits brought me to this exact block. I remember standing in line for two hours outside the New York Theater Workshop, hoping that, by some small miracle, we'd get tickets to see the original company of *Rent*, its gritty legend already well-established. I didn't actually get to see it until a few years later, when I was terribly disappointed by the flashy touring cast.

Then, there's the beautiful skinny townhouse that holds the LaMama Experimental Café. I visited my friend Andrea at this townhouse one evening. She'd met LaMama founder Ellen Stewart at a conference in San Diego and was invited to stay at the theater when she visited. We explored the building's every nook and cranny and met crazy Hungarian circus performers. Andrea's room was literally a closet, large enough for a single bed and a nightstand. And short on cash, we passed the evening sipping tea by the large windows, talking about our dreams, and watching the snowfall.

Across the street, at 85 East Fourth, a small neon sign illuminated the dark-blue afternoon with three very recognizable red letters: K-G-B. I walked up the steep stoop steps, opened the big red doors, and entered a small, rundown lobby with unpolished floors and paint peeling off the high tin ceilings. A very steep staircase ascended two flights in one stretch toward the back of the building. On the other side of the little lobby were two doors. One said "The Kraine Theater," the other said "Office." I knocked on the door marked "Office."

"Who is it?" a voice asked.

"Hi. My name is Randy Anderson. I'd like to talk to someone about renting a theater." The door opened, and an unshaven man peered out at me.

"Which theater?"

"I don't know. You have more than one?"

"Yeah, we have three: the Kraine, the Red Room, and Under St. Marks. Which one are you interested in?"

The man still hadn't fully opened the door, and I heard someone giggling. Was there a girl in there? Was she dressed?

"If I'm interrupting something, I can come back later," I said, stepping back.

"Which theater did you want to look at? Somebody's in the Kraine right now, but the Red Room is open. You can go up and take a look, if you want." The hidden person was laughing now, which made me a bit insecure. "Just go all the way up to the top of those stairs and make a right, first door on your left. If you have any questions, give us a knock on your way out." And he began to close the door.

"Great. Thanks. And your name is?"

"Russell."

"Super. Thanks, Russell." And he closed the door to the sounds of even more laughter. Chris told me these people were laid-back, but this Russell guy struck me as a little cagey.

I started up the marble stairs. Halfway up was a landing and, to the right, the entrance to the KGB bar. A quick glance showed a dark room with candlelit tables, windows covered with heavy red drapes, and walls adorned with old communist propaganda. A few couples sat around in quiet conversations, and I couldn't help but fantasize they were real communists, plotting something. What that something was I couldn't imagine, since I'd only been conditioned, as a child, to believe communists plotted. No one ever said what about. The bartender looked up at me, and I responded with a smile and a wave, which felt silly. Communist don't wave and smile, right? They're serious people. The bartender acknowledged me with a nod, and I continued up the stairs.

Now out of breath, I finally arrived at the top. It was poorly lit, but I managed to find the unmarked theater. I opened the door and looked into complete darkness. I reached my hand inside and felt along the wall for a light switch without success. The little bit of light spilling in from the hallway revealed rows of chairs sloping up. Behind the last row, I made out a square hole, cut into the wall. The technical booth! I was sure to find a way to illuminate the theater there.

After propping the door open with a nearby garbage can, I slowly walked into the room and up the aisle toward the booth. I made it halfway up when I heard the garbage can fall over and the door close, immediately leaving me enveloped in darkness. Not even an illuminated exit sign offered its dim glow. Pausing for a moment to determine whether to continue to the booth or go back and re-prop the door, I got on all fours and crawled forward on the dusty floor. Messy jeans and dirty hands beat tripping on the unknown.

Finally, at the top of the risers, I followed some cables to the booth. Once inside, I reached into my pocket and pulled out my lighter. One flick lit up the booth. The small flame provided just enough light for me to read the masking-tape labels identifying the various controls. I passed the lighter over the controls systematically from left to right and located a circular dimmer labeled "house." I cranked the knob to the right, and the house lights came on.

Considering the amount of dust in the air, I was lucky the place didn't blow up when I lit my lighter. I stepped onto the stage and felt an immediate thrill. It was a black-box theater, cozy, small, and in decent condition. The lights hung from a grid just below the tin ceilings, and I immediately noticed the lack of air conditioning. I spent a good 20 minutes wandering around the small room. There wasn't that much to see, but I've always loved being alone in a theater. It feeds my creativity.

Standing in the audience staring at the stage, I see a son throw his fists down on the kitchen counter while his mother sobs about his unexpected news. I see a passionate kiss between a couple who have just discovered their love for each other and know they'll soon be separated forever. I see a drunken punch, the final spin of a dance, the maniacal laugh of a tormented clown. I see the lights go down then come up for the cast's final bow. The events that transpire on the stage, even in my imagination, are immediate and in the moment. No place else on earth gives me such imaginative powers as an empty theater. And imagining myself covered in a beggar's fairy dust, I sprinted down the stairs to the office.

I knocked on the office door. "Russell, it's Randy." I waited a moment but didn't hear anything. "I looked at the space and I want to talk to you about some dates."

Finally, Russell opened the door and a billow of marijuana smoke curled itself into the fresh lobby air. Suddenly, all the giggling and caginess made sense.

"Come on in!" Russell said with a big grin as he shook my hand and pulled me into the tiny office, where we worked out the details of a three-day rental in June. Russell had only recently started renting out the theaters. He and a few other guys had started this company called Horse Trade, and he spoke at great length about how they were going to improve the spaces and, most importantly, bring them up to code. We went over the one-page contract, which stipulated a $500 deposit. When I pulled out my credit card, Russell stared at me.

"You don't have cash?" he asked. Since moving to New York, I'd grown accustomed to using cash more often, but 500 dollars seemed a ridiculous request.

"No, I don't even have 500 dollars in my bank account. I was hoping I could put this on my credit card."

In retrospect, it was probably a bad idea to disclose the fact I didn't have any money, but Russell didn't seem to mind. We talked about how I was going to finance the project, and he agreed to let me pay in installments.

"Here, let's seal the deal," Russell said, offering me his pipe.

I walked back out into the street, where the fall air smelled better than ever.

When I got back to the bar, Chris was sitting at our earlier table with our friends, Andrea and Deborah.

"Hi, gang!" I said. "Andrea, I was just thinking about you when I walked passed LaMama. I'm going to grab a drink. Does anyone need anything?"

There was a slight wobble in my step and a silly half-grin on my face.

"We're good," Chris said. "So what happened? You look stoned. Are you stoned?"

Being a stoner, Chris was very perceptive about these things.

"No man. I'm fine. Hold on a moment, let me get a drink."

I swerved to the bar and ordered a Brooklyn Lager, feeling particularly good—and not just because of the pot. Reserving the theater had emboldened my confidence and tapped a reservoir of ambition that was awaiting direction. I'm the kind of person who always capitalizes on moments of confidence, so by the time I carried my beer back to the table, my three-night play grew into something much, much larger.

"Andrea, Deborah, what's going on?" I asked as I set my beer down and took my seat.

"Nothing much going on with us," said Deborah, staring at me.

"Is there something going on with you?" Andrea asked.

They were all looking at me with such intensity, I couldn't tell if I was paranoid or pretty.

"There *is* something going on with me," I baited. "I've just started working on a project."

"What project?" Andrea inquired.

"Did you book the space?" Chris asked impatiently.

"Yes. I've booked the space." I raised my glass, and everyone else followed suit. "And I'm starting a theater company," I said triumphantly.

"What!" Chris exclaimed.

"Awesome!" Deborah said.

"I just booked the Red Room Theater for three nights in June for the world premier of my new play, *Testing Average*."

It was a very grand way of saying, "I'm doing a little play in a little theater." But we write who we are by the words we use, and at that moment, I was starting a theater company that would be mounting a world-premier play!

"That is so fucking exciting!" Andrea exclaimed. "Here's to a new theater company."

We touched glasses, drank, and immediately started getting lost in the possibilities. Then, Chris put his beer on the table.

"What's this company going to be called?" he asked.

I hadn't thought about a company name. For the contract, I had signed only my own name.

Retreating into my mind, I searched for ideas. But the idea wasn't hidden deep in the clefts of my brain. It was all over my face, head, and clothes: self-reflection taking the form of a white dust cast onto me by a beggar.

"The Beggars Group," I replied with certainty.

It was in my head and out of my mouth in an instant. Usually, that kind of spontaneity gets me into trouble, but this time, it had a positive effect. The Beggars Group was the name of the theater company and the kind of theater the company would produce—theater that makes people look at themselves a little closer, as contemplative entertainment.

"To The Beggars Group!" Chris said, raising his glass once more.

"To The Beggars Group!" we all responded as we knocked glasses and drank. I'd found my direction, and it was no different from when I was 10. It's funny how we can find our direction, lose it, and then find it again. I suppose one's direction in life, like success, is a fluid concept. We settled into our stools and exchanged ideas as twilight faded and East Fourth Street darkened, turning the glow of the pub into a beacon for dreamers and drunks.

TESTING AVERAGE

Twenty-five minutes before show time, the audience was so far pretty light. We'd only just opened the house, and I was petrified nobody would show up. The past six months had been at once thrilling and exhausting, but I had done it. I'd managed to write, direct, and produce my first show in New York.

Chris didn't exactly lie about the show not costing me an arm and a leg, but it did cost more than I had budgeted. Foolishly, I assumed renting the theater would be my largest expense, but I hadn't anticipated the other piece of real estate I'd need: rehearsal space. A rehearsal room large enough for a cast of 10 cost $20 to $25 an hour, which could easily add up to more than $1,000. Since I didn't have that kind of money, I booked the few hours I could afford, and we headed to Central Park for the rest of rehearsals.

Rehearsing in New York parks is not that uncommon. Walk through Central Park on a nice day, and you'll see all kinds of artists practicing their crafts privately in a public space. Shakespeare, Chekhov, juggling, dance...it's all there for your enjoyment. The actors were a little hesitant at first. Sure, it's not the ideal rehearsal venue, but producing theater on a shoestring is sadly familiar territory for most thespians—at least all the thespians in my cast. Everyone in *Testing Average* was a personal friend. Bobby, Chris, Deborah, Andrea, and a few other acquaintances were all now safely in the dressing room, preparing to dazzle our audience.

"Hello, my love!" said a beautiful Jamaican woman as she fought through the heavy metal doors. It was my friend Donna accompanied by two other co-workers from Blah-Blah Big Bank.

"Donna, I'm so glad you made it!"

"Are you kidding? I wouldn't miss it for the world. Here..." she said handing me 40 dollars. "This is for the three of us."

"Let me get you some change," I said as I plunged into my strongbox.

"Nonsense, you keep the change. Where do we go? Is it right here?" She pointed to the first-floor theater.

"No, you actually have to go up those stairs."

"All the way up? Oh, you're kidding me. Good thing I skipped the gym today."

"Yes, but you can stop at the bar half way up and get a drink."

"Excellent! That will give us some incentive!" she laughed and exchanged jokes with her two partners-in-crime as they ascended the stairs. While she wasn't a theater person, she had, in a way, collaborated with me on the show's set.

One Tuesday afternoon at Blah-Blah Big Bank, Donna and I went out to lunch. I loved lunching with Donna because her stories—especially the recent ones about her and her husband's adventures with a group of swingers—made for an entertaining hour. As we finished our bento boxes and plum wine, I told her about my set issues. Contractually, we couldn't create a permanent set. Throughout the week, a multitude of productions used the venue. A weekend night could have a show at 8, one at 10:30, and yet another at midnight. That gave us little time to load-in and load-out—and limited space for storage. Thankfully, *Testing Average* required only two main sets: six classroom desks and chairs and a dining-room table.

I explained all this to Donna, hoping a brilliant solution would appear from our empty plum-wine glasses. After we paid the check, Donna grabbed me by the hand.

"Come on," she began in her thick Jamaican accent. "I know just the thing for you. Have you been to Odd Lots?"

"Odd Lots? Never heard of it. Is it some kind of swingers' club for misfits?" I asked, smiling as she dragged me through the busy midtown streets.

"Don't be fresh with me, Mr. Anderson. Come on, you're gonna love this."

Donna was persistent, direct, and a little pushy. I loved it. If I had liked the ladies, and she actually *did* swing, our relationship could have been quite different. But I was content to be the gay sidekick following her magnificent figure through the aisles of what appeared to be a dollar store.

"Get that horrified expression off your face. I know what you're thinking, but you can find really good deals here."

Surrounded by cheap lawn ornaments, plastic barrels of generic cheese puffs, and children-sized underwear with "Foxy Girl" written in glitter on the crotch, I let her confidence assuage my cynicism.

"Here we are," said Donna, taking off her jacket and placing it over a clothes rack full of tiger pajamas with plush tails. "First, you need six of these." She pulled out six folding TV dinner trays. "Open them up! Don't just stand there like a lost child."

I sprung into action.

"And six of these," she continued, as she took out six small folding stools. Within a minute, Donna had set up the tables and chairs in a row. "See? You can make rows of desks like this for a classroom."

Then, she pushed the TV trays together, three and three, and threw a tablecloth she had grabbed from somewhere over them.

"Now, you have a dinner table!" It was brilliant in its simplicity.

"That's perfect, Donna! How much does all this cost?" I asked, still skeptical.

"The TV trays are three dollars each, and the stools are four. So, we'll say 45 bucks with tax."

"Perfect!" I exclaimed. "You're brilliant. I'm gonna come back on Friday when I get paid and pick these up."

I was beginning to walk out, but Donna grabbed my arm.

"What, are you crazy? You can't wait until Friday. These won't be here on Friday. Dear, this is Odd Lots. Things sell out quickly."

"You mean to tell me these tiger pajamas with the plush tails will be gone by the end of the week?"

"No, those will be here, but these trays and stools won't. I promise you. Here, let me buy them. You can pay me back on Friday."

That was her last word on the subject. I protested, she insisted, and I had a set.

Fifteen minutes before show time, a slow-but-steady parade of patrons marched up the stairs. Most were the performers' friends, dressed for a Friday night and far too nice for this dirty little theater. A woman, who must have been about 70, managed to pull the red doors open just enough to slide her thin frame through.

"Is this the Red Room Theater?" she asked in a shockingly loud voice.

"Yes, it is," I replied. "Are you here to see *Testing Average*?"

"Is that the play Justin is in?"

She pulled out a crumpled square of paper that instantly embarrassed me when I recognized it as our postcard. I didn't know this woman, but I didn't want her first impression of the company to be this pitiful postcard.

Not terribly strong with publicity, I had no idea how to effectively promote a super-short run of a new play by an unknown playwright produced by a brand new theater company. And while postcards are remarkably cheap to print if you want five thousand of them, I only had three performances. So, a four-digit print job seemed like overkill. Instead, Bobby and I mocked up a design on his computer and color-copied the postcards at our local photocopy place. The quality was terrible. And here was Grandma, unfolding this crookedly cut piece of cardstock and pointing to Justin's name.

"I'm in an acting class with him," she said, which explained the tremendous voice. "Do I get a discount?"

"I'm sorry, ma'am. There are no discounts."

I wasn't sure if she felt she deserved a discount because she was a friend or because she was old, but she'll get Social Security, which probably won't exist by the time I retire. She scowled a little, handed me a 10-dollar bill, and looked up the stairs.

"I have to go up there?"

"Yes, ma'am, I'm afraid there is no elevator."

"Jesus fucking Christ! First you make me pay full price, then you make me climb these stairs. What kind of crappy operation is this?" She began her slow climb, muttering to herself. "Now, where are my tissues?"

We now had more than 20 people in the theater, and I had 300 dollars in my strongbox. I relaxed a little. Two more nights like this, and I'd break even. C.J. came in next with two friends but no flowers. Considering how these two friends felt about me, I was surprised to see the friends; and considering how C.J. felt about me, I was surprised to see no flowers.

"So, are you excited?" he asked, flashing his crooked grin that sent his lower lip toward his chin. I was so taken by this lopsided smile.

"Yeah! Here you go!" I handed them their programs. C.J.'s friends begrudgingly handed me their money and headed up the stairs. C.J. looked uncomfortable.

"Are you OK?" I asked. "You seem nervous."

"I am! This is your big debut! Aren't *you* nervous?"

"Are you kidding me? I'm freaking out! But it's gonna be good, so I'm excited, too. I hope you like it."

I hadn't shared any of the play with him. He only knew what it was about, nothing more. He'd asked me, on several occasions, to include him in the writing process, but I didn't allow it. Like the adage, "don't shit where you eat," mine was, "don't create where you copulate."

"I was going to bring you flowers," he said, "but I thought you wouldn't like to have to carry them around all night."

He was terribly wrong and even more wrong for saying that. I think it was because *he* didn't want to carry them around all night. I suppose a boy giving another boy flowers is still somehow awkward in our society, but I love flowers and wished I had some for my opening night.

"Don't worry about it. And stop being nervous. It's out of our hands. Let the actors be nervous." I sent him upstairs to join his friends.

"We're at five!" shouted Lolly from upstairs. "Hi, C.J.!"

I didn't see her greet my boyfriend, but I knew it was our stage manager.

Finding technical staff was far more difficult than I first thought. Luckily, the four moveable lights in the Red Room reduced our lighting design from a "job" to a "favor," which Big Rob gladly granted. But I was hard-pressed to find a stage manager, the cornerstone position for any production. My several attempts to bring in an experienced stage manager at a salary of zero brought me no takers. Nor did any friends volunteer, so I recruited a friend of a friend, who had no idea what the job entailed. Thankfully, the flawed idea that a warm body was better than no body would never be tested. Lolly arrived just in time.

One week before the show, as we began technical rehearsals, I was gleefully burning the candle at both ends. My schedule included nine hours at Blah-Blah Big Bank, four hours in rehearsal, and three hours at the bar. I certainly could have cut those days shorter by skipping the bar, but that was actually the most productive part of my day. A great deal of business would happen in those dark-wooden dens. Talking through issues with the show, drumming up an audience, brainstorming future projects, or simply blowing off steam all happened in the magical hours just before and after midnight. But even at 24 years young, this schedule exhausted me.

As the rest of the group made their transition to performers, I recognized I was going to be left in the house without a stage manager. Thankfully, three days before opening, Lolly walked through the door.

"What the fuck, dudes?" shouted the tall radiant woman in no particular direction. "Let's make some theater!"

"Lolly!" I exclaimed, leaping out of my chair.

"Oh, there you are. I heard you were putting on a show. Let's make some theater! What do you need?"

Lolly was a good friend of mine from college. A fantastic actress with an offbeat artistic sensibility, she was easily the wildest, most adventurous redhead I knew. She had just moved to the city after spending the last three years in a graduate acting program in the middle of nowhere America.

"I'm afraid the show is cast already," I said. "Too bad you didn't graduate a month ago."

"No shit. Seriously, what do you need? I don't care what you have me do. I'll do anything. I just wanna work."

So, I relieved the petrified friend of a friend behind the light board, and Lolly got to work.

"Randy, close down the box, get the fuck up here, and let's do a show!" Lolly shouted down over the noise of the KGB patrons.

The moment had arrived. I closed the strongbox, put it under my arm, took a breath, and sprinted up the stairs two at a time.

When I walked into the Red Room Theater, it evoked a whole different energy from when I first crawled into its darkness last fall. Yet somehow, it wasn't unfamiliar. I had visualized this moment so many times in the past eight months that seeing it for real felt oddly repetitive.

It turns out it's not hard to make a 30-seat theater look full. And with a cast of 10, family and friends fill the place quickly. Only a few seats remained. Lolly had placed a stool for me next to the booth, and I greeted people as I walked up the aisle. Then, I took my seat.

Looking out over the audience, I became instantly addicted to the feeling of putting on a show in the East Village. I loved seeing my co-workers from Blah-Blah Big Bank settling into their seats, drinks in hand, taking in the bohemian experience. I listened for a minute to strangers talking about what they knew about the show or whom they knew in it. And then the house lights dimmed, the conversations quieted, the programs settled, and my little story about success began.

PEACH PASTRIES

After the short-but-sweet success of *Testing Average*, The Beggars, as we now called ourselves, began meeting on a regular basis. Realizing I could no longer do all the work myself, six of us—Lolly, Bobby, Andrea, Deborah, Kathy, and I—banded together to create a company of producers. One of our favorite places to assemble was the Hungarian Pastry Shop. Nestled on the Upper West Side, it's a cozy café filled with excellent coffee, yummy pastries, and Ivy League students discussing Nietzsche.

Lolly and I, the first to arrive at 10 a.m. on this particular Saturday morning, secured a table in the back, ordered coffee, tea, and a dozen peach jelly–filled pastries.

"So, I think we have an idea for a great show," Lolly started with excitement.

"Let's hear it," I replied.

But Lolly wouldn't divulge anything until the others arrived. Lolly is at her best when she's coy. She squints her eyes and gets a smirk on her lips that signals fun. Bobby stumbled in past the front counter.

"I need some coffee!" he said too loudly to the woman behind the counter. She politely took his order and told him to have a seat. Seeing our waves from the back, he stumbled his way to our table.

"Why are we meeting so fucking early?" He hadn't come home the night before, so he was obviously sleep-deprived.

"It's 10," Lolly said. "It's not early. You just went to bed too late."

"Ha! What makes you think I went to bed?" Bobby said with a laugh. "Where are The Girls?"

We'd taken to calling Andrea, Deborah, and Kathy "The Girls," as Lolly aligned herself more closely to us boys.

"They'll be here soon," I replied. "They're all coming from Queens."

"Fucking Queens," Rob exclaimed.

"Fucking Queens," Lolly repeated. "Who the fuck lives in Queens anyway?"

"I don't know, a couple million people, maybe?" I said.

We definitely had a bias against the boroughs. As if cued, The Girls paraded into the café, settled into their seats, and our powwow began.

The Girls and Lolly immediately launched into their idea for a play based on the life of Zelda Fitzgerald, wife of writer F. Scott Fitzgerald and, as The Girls quickly pointed out, a writer in her own right. She had written a posthumously published book, they reported, called

Save Me the Waltz. After they confirmed Zelda's own artistry, they turned to the details of her glamorous yet tortured life.

Every bit a southern belle, Zelda agreed to marry Scott only after he published his first novel, *This Side of Paradise*, and then, only if it was a success. Once his promising career was established, they wed and immediately took New York by storm. Riding on the tops of cabs, jumping into fountains, dancing and drinking the nights away, they quickly became the king and queen of the roaring '20s.

Bobby and I asked questions, and books piled up on the table. Lolly and The Girls spared no detail of their extensive research. The Fitzgeralds spent far too much money keeping up their expensive lifestyle and needed a cheaper alternative to New York. Still recovering from World War I, Paris—an inexpensive cosmopolitan city filled with expatriate artists living cheaply and living large—was far more accommodating to the Fitzgeralds' level of consumption.

Everyone who was anyone lived in Paris in those days. The Fitzgeralds passed their time with the likes of Ernest Hemingway, Gertrude Stein, and Sara and Gerald Murphy. We could see why Lolly and The Girls were so excited about this fascinating collection of artistic giants.

Their play would capture the energy of the period while looking at the under-examined talent of Zelda. As they saw it, history had relegated her artistic contributions to a mere footnote. I wasn't convinced we should construct an entire play focusing on a woman few people had heard of, but the idea of making a play about the 1920s felt like a good direction.

The year 1999 may as well have been 1928. The '90s were already being heralded as the second Gilded Age. The freewheeling, easy-living attitude was a carbon copy of the late '20s, when money and jobs were also plentiful. It felt timely. By exploring the past, we could illuminate the present. We could even be prophetic! After all, the Roaring '20s were followed by the Great Depression. And while nobody was talking about a Depression in 1999, I was convinced the thought was lurking somewhere deep inside our society's collective subconscious.

"So, was Zelda crazy?" asked Bobby, looking up from a book he was scanning.

"What do you mean by crazy?" Andrea asked.

"Well, it says here, she died in a fire at an insane asylum where she was a patient," he said, pointing at the page he was reading. This immediately peaked my interest.

"You mean to say, not only was she crazy, like wild-party crazy, but she was also insane-crazy?" I asked with excitement.

"No, she wasn't insane," said Deborah sternly. "She had some mental problems, but she wasn't insane."

I was struck by how defensive The Girls got about Zelda. Even Lolly objected to my accusation. I wasn't sure if it was because I called Zelda insane or the obvious delight I took in the idea, but either way, they were not going to tolerate my insulting her.

"Come on," I said. "Nothing makes for better drama than someone going insane."

"Well, we don't want to make a play about Zelda going insane," said Andrea, attempting to put the conversation back on track.

"But why not?" I continued. "I mean, if she went insane, we should capitalize on that! Even if she didn't go insane, I think we should make her go insane."

Bobby nodded in agreement. Of all people, he understood the whole "insane person as entertainment" thing. He made a point of being insane for that very reason.

"We can't just make stuff up," Deborah said. "We have to be true to the research."

That moved us past deliberating on the degree of Zelda's mental illness into a very profound discussion on the type of play this would be. The Girls had clearly done much research. They wanted to explore every nook and cranny of this woman's life. I had no problem with that, but I insisted we avoid creating a "bio-play." Historical facts could serve as a launching pad, but I wanted allegory, symbolism, and universal themes. I wanted to present these people's lives in a fantastical world filled with high drama and stunning visuals.

In order to achieve this, we were going to have to make things up. Historical reality would read too flat. The Girls didn't agree. They believed Zelda's reality was fantastical enough. And I suppose, for them, it was.

I couldn't know it then, but Zelda's reality would eventually make a mess out of mine. That argument clearly wasn't going to get solved over peach pastries, so

I suggested we table that conversation and look at possible titles for the piece.

"I don't think we can title the project yet," Kathy said.

My head fell into my hands. "Fucking artists," I thought to myself. This was the price I had to pay for creating a group—discussion and compromise. And I wouldn't always mind it, but sometimes I'd have to resort to manipulation.

"Yeah," agreed Andrea. "The title will come later. We need to develop the idea further."

I paused and bit my cheek.

"Why don't we discuss possible titles for the piece? Maybe we'll develop the idea further," I said very diplomatically.

"I don't know," said Kathy, shaking her head. Lolly, Bobby, and Deborah quietly picked at the remaining sweets on the table.

"Well, I do," I said, punctuating my declaration with a sip of coffee, pinky down. "Let's brainstorm and see what we come up with. We don't have to choose anything now. Think of it as an exercise."

I knew we'd be walking away from this meeting with a title. Would it be the final title, I couldn't know, but we'd be digesting our pastries calling this project something.

A project doesn't exist until it has a title. I know it may sound ridiculous because clearly, it does exist without a title. Like a shoe. Even if there were no word for shoe, a shoe still exists. But I can't live in a world where you need to tie "that thing on your feet." When someone asks me what project The Beggars Group is working on, I need to be able to say "SHOE."

"So how about *Save the Last Waltz*?" I started

"No," Andrea said. "That's the title of her book, and we're not doing her book. How about just *Zelda*?"

The brainstorming began. Everyone had ideas, and the dialogue moved from a jovial competition of cleverness to full-blown discussions about characters. We started to build the core of the play. Ernest Hemingway, F. Scott and Zelda Fitzgerald, Sara and Gerald Murphy would all grace the stage in our pageantry of people past. They all had at least one thing in common: They were all American expatriates living in Paris in the 1920s. They were expatriates. The play was about the expatriates. The play would be called *The Expatriates*.

Once we hit that word, the conversation exploded. "Expatriates" is loaded with a million thematic applications, and it officially became the title of the project.

"What are you working on?" people would ask.

"The Expatriates," I'd say, and launch into the tagline, followed by the detailed description.

As the afternoon sun grew heavy, we established a timeline for this opus. We would submit the project to FringeNYC, the largest downtown theater festival in the city, for the summer of 2000. After this workshop production, we would rework the play and present a full run in the fall, two months later. We were excited by the challenge of this extreme ambition. A little over a year to write the piece seemed a comfortable amount of time to really dig into these people's lives.

As if that wasn't enough, a few side projects were put on the table as well. The Beggars Group was a new muscle we'd all just discovered, and we were eager to flex it. The more we produced, the better we'd become at it, and the more people would know about us. So while our main artistic creation was a year away, we had a litany of projects to help raise our profile and sharpen our skills.

We would produce Charles Busch's *Theodora, She Bitch of Byzantium*, an evening of music by Stephanie, and an experimental poetry piece curated by Andrea. There seemed to be no end to the theatrical evenings we could generate. And generating art was like rocket fuel for our ambitions, propelling us to do more. We filtered out of the café seven hours after we had arrived, jacked up on caffeine, with clear goals and ambitious hearts.

AUNT PHYLLIS

One of our biggest challenges was how to fund all this ambition. My handy credit card, which I wasn't afraid to use, didn't provide a realistic, long-term strategy. We started a solicitation campaign and scheduled a few fund-raising parties. And while those 20-dollar donations added up quickly, we needed larger infusions of cash. So, everyone else got to work on grant research, and I got to work on courting a benefactor.

I met my Great-Aunt Phyllis at a private club on the Upper East Side. She had flown in from San Francisco for a few days, and we were going to have lunch at the club and then head to the theater. Aunt Phyllis, who is my father's aunt, was the only living relation on his side of the family. Her life was steeped in mystery. While her vibrancy belied her 80 years on this earth, her sophistication and manners were undoubtedly from an earlier era. Eager to hear her thoughts on the literary giants we were studying, I arrived wearing suit and tie as requested.

"Well, hello!" Aunt Phyllis said warmly, as I entered the unassuming building into an elegant lobby adorned with dark wood beams and gold trim. "I trust you didn't have any difficulty finding this place."

"No troubles at all," I said. "Once you know the grid, everything is easy to find in Manhattan." And we embraced.

"Wonderful, then, let's get some lunch."

Aunt Phyllis led the way to the dining room. The century-old building was immaculate. The lobby ceiling rose three stories high, and a second-floor balcony hung like a halo at the top of a grand staircase. I imagined F. Scott and Zelda having a spectacular fight on the stairs for an audience of robber barons and their mistresses. We walked under the stairs and into the restaurant, where the tuxedoed maître'd showed us to our seats.

I didn't know why Aunt Phyllis had come to New York. When I asked her on the phone, she brushed off the question, saying she had "things to take care of." Was that true or did she want to check in on me? No matter the reason, I was glad to see her. While on the phone, we had spoken about The Beggars Group, and I had introduced the idea of her contributing. Now, I wanted to make a formal solicitation in person.

"So, let's talk about your theater career," she started, as we dove into our gazpacho. "Are you still going out on auditions?"

"No," I said. "I'm really focusing on building this theater company."

"Well, isn't that exciting!" Aunt Phyllis exclaimed, using her popular phrase that always seemed to precede a critique. "I don't suppose you're going to make much money doing that, though."

"No," I said again. "But I'm making enough money at Blah-Blah Big Bank."

"Yes, well, I'm sure you are. But you don't want to be a banker, do you? That doesn't really interest you. Don't you want to make a living doing something you enjoy?"

My instinct was to say "yes," but that's a trap. Phyllis was full of these traps. Once I agree, she'll insist the path I'm on won't get me to where I need to be.

When Lolly and I had stayed with her in San Francisco to audition for graduate schools, she kept insisting an actor had no need for a graduate degree.

"If you want to be an actor," she said, "I would think you should just go out and act."

"This coming from a woman who has her MBA!" I argued. "Did people tell you that if you wanted to be a businesswoman, you should skip school and go out and do business?"

"Don't be ridiculous. When I told people I wanted to be in business, they laughed at me and sent me for coffee. That was a different time. There weren't many women in the workplace. But anyway, that's business. Anybody who's serious about business gets an MBA. Acting... well, I don't know much about it, but I would think that spending three years of your youth at some university is not the way to make a career. People want young actors. This is the time you should be out there trying to make it!"

Lolly and I tried our best to explain to her the virtues of a graduate acting degree, but she wouldn't have it. Lolly ended up getting accepted and I did not, so we would see in 10 years which route was best.

"Yes," I started, as I pushed the empty soup bowl away. "I do want to make a living doing something I enjoy, but if I'm going to truly do what I want to do, which is make theater, I'm going to have to build it slowly. I'm not interested in going out on auditions all the time. I don't have the stomach for that kind of life."

"Well, how do you expect to be an actor if you don't go out on auditions?" Aunt Phyllis sparred.

She was so unbelievably good-natured when she asked direct questions, and I'm sure that's how she achieved her level of success.

"Yes, you're right," I conceded, so I could change the direction of the conversation. "So, about my theater company..."

My introduction may have been weak, but the prospect of "the ask" made me uncomfortable and inarticulate.

"Wait, are you saying I'm right just to get off the subject?" she interrupted.

"I am, I'm sorry," I said sheepishly. "I forgot you weren't born yesterday."

"More like 29 thousand yesterdays," she said, which totally disarmed me as I ran calculations in my head to check her accuracy. We should all have minds this sharp at 80.

"Yes! Your theater company! I'll stop grilling you for now. Let's talk about this exciting endeavor! I have a check for you. Don't let me forget to give it to you."

And just like that, "the ask" and "the receive" were over. I instantly relaxed.

"Well, thank you very much," I said, as our second course arrived. "That's going to be a great help."

"I want to help," she said.

"Thank you," I repeated and launched into my pitch about *The Expatriates*.

She listened intently. Being only 20 years younger than our characters, she had a working knowledge of their lives and firsthand memories of the Depression. I pitched the show pretty hard, even though she had already agreed to give us money. I wanted her to feel good about her investment, but I also wanted to comb her mind for any lurking details about that era.

"Well, isn't that exciting!" Aunt Phyllis said after I finished. "But I'm not sure about the name."

"Well, the play is really about expatriation so..." I started, braced to defend our name.

"No, not the play. The play sounds wonderful. And I love the title. *The Expatriates* sounds exotic and exciting. I don't care for the name of the company."

My spine collapsed into a lower-case "c." I loved the name The Beggars Group. I called myself a "Beggar." It was already infused with my identity.

"Well, the name speaks to the experience we want the audience to have when they see our shows," I said passionately. "Seeing a beggar on the street causes you to self-reflect."

"I don't know about that," said Aunt Phyllis, taking a bite of salad. "I just think that if you want people to give you money, you should have a name that says 'success.' People like giving money to successful projects. The Beggars Group doesn't sound successful. You don't want to be beggars. You want to be emperors. How about The Emperors Group?"

The Emperors Group? It sounded like a place you went to for high-end hookers.

"Well, I don't think the Emperors Group is exactly what we're going for."

I could see her point, but I was convinced this was a generational thing.

"We want to convey an everyman feeling. You know. We don't want to come across as elitist."

"Why not?" Aunt Phyllis asked. "This club is elitist. There's nothing wrong with being elitist. But if it bothers you to think of it as elitism, then think of it as excellence. Only the smartest get into Yale. Only the brightest are published in the *Harvard Law Review*. Only the best are in The Emperors Group."

Chuckling at the name, I nodded my head.

"Beggars may not be the best or the brightest, but they're genuine," I said.

"I suppose you're right."

My joy in her acceptance tempered as I waited for the inevitable twist in logic.

"And may your theater be gracious enough to allow us to see it."

She raised her iced tea in my direction. And I finished my pesto chicken sandwich wondering if she had agreed with me simply to get off the subject.

After lunch, we went to see *Wit* in Union Square. Whenever we got together, Aunt Phyllis would take me to the theater and let me pick the show. Unfortunately, my youthful passion to explore the depths of life and death never sat well with her 80-year-old sensibilities. As smart and worldly as she was, she'd pick a musical comedy over more serious fare any day. Unless it was Shakespeare. She loved good Shakespeare.

My choice for this visit, *Wit* is about a woman dying of cancer. Moved by the experience, I left the theater transformed in some foreign and exciting way.

"Well… that was depressing," said Aunt Phyllis, looking at me lovingly with a hint of sadness.

I would see this sadness in her every now an then, usually when her guard was down. And I suppose nothing gets your guard down like a good play about death. Although I couldn't identify the origin of this sadness, there was a long list of possibilities. She had lived through the Depression, World War II, her friends dying at an accelerated rate, and now this totally depressing play I suddenly deeply regretted suggesting. Maybe she was sad because our date was ending? Maybe she was still disappointed because I named my theater company The Beggars Group? I would never know because, as Aunt Phyllis would say, "It's just not something you talk about," and I'm too polite to pry. We both acknowledged the sadness in silence.

I folded out my elbow and Aunt Phyllis clutched it as we walked across Union Square Park. The sounds of buskers and political activists rang out from its south side. We made a small detour to listen to the protestors but didn't join them. We weren't going to free Tibet tonight.

"I've been to Tibet," Aunt Phyllis said quietly. "They should be free."

I knew very little about the subject but quickly agreed. "Everybody should be free."

"Well, the people of Tibet should be. That's all I know. There's my cab."

She threw her fingers up and pointed as if she'd been expecting that very cab to pick her up at that very moment. I hugged and kissed her. As she got into the car, she pressed a $1,000 check into my hands. "Best of luck dear. It's going to be wonderful. I just know it."

"Thank you, Aunt Phyllis," I said as I shut the door.

And I watched the taillights of her cab disappear into a sea of flickering red lights slowly moving uptown.

ROCK AND ROLL

"So I want us to think of this play as rock-and-roll," Chris told us. "It's going to be late, the audience is coming in from the bar downstairs with drinks in hand, and they're gonna be pumped. We'll be blasting some crazy music as they take their seats, and when the lights go down, I want the play to pop with so much energy, the audience thinks they're watching a fucking rock concert!"

He finished with his fists in the air, and we cheered, ready to take on the concept. Who wouldn't be? Doesn't everyone want to be a rock-and-roll star?

Chris was directing Charles Busch's *Theodora, She Bitch of Byzantium*, The Beggars Group's late-night offering at the Red Room Theater. *Theodora, She Bitch of Byzantium,* is a short, wildly entertaining piece about the campy adventures of a Byzantine emperor's wife.

I had booked the 10:30 p.m. slot in the Red Room Theater every Saturday for eight weeks. The Girls set to work securing the rights to perform the play, a task that turned out to be far more difficult than we initially thought. Because Charles Busch was working on another project uptown, there was some question about whether our little-known group should be granted production rights to *Theodora, She Bitch of Byzantium*.

If we were in Topeka or Minneapolis or Key West or anywhere else in the country, we would have had no problem. Hell, if we were producing the show across the river in New Jersey, we'd have had the rights in a heartbeat. But New York has its own rules. It is the country's theatrical capital and as such, authors and agents are far more scrutinizing when granting rights permission. Thankfully, The Girls' tenacity convinced the agency that, despite our $2,000 budget, we would present the play in the most professional manner.

"Yeah, we'll show them professional," Chris said after learning we got the rights. "Professional rock-and-roll!"

And he unfurled a beautifully painted muslin backdrop of a vagina with a slit through the middle for our upstage center entrance. Girl power is a huge theme in the play, and Chris wanted to make sure everyone in the audience understood that. So, just in case we performers didn't get that across, there'd always be the giant labia on stage.

Besides this backdrop, we needed no other set pieces, which gave me a great sigh of relief. Getting in and out of this show would be much easier without set pieces—or so I thought.

With no set to worry about, we turned our attention to creating Theodora. I'd done this part in college, but now, I was keenly aware that doing drag in the East Village required a much greater eye for detail. In New York, drag is a profession. Here, people put "drag performer" on their tax forms. I couldn't just throw some apples in a bra, slip on a dress, slap on some makeup, and parade around. I needed to *bring* it.

We combed some downtown thrift shops and found me a slinky purple gown and open-toed, two-inch heels. That left the wig and the makeup.

In rehearsals, I had been prancing in my heels and a secondhand, misshapen wig as if I'd done it my whole life. But the real wig, our performance wig, had thus far eluded us.

The subject of my makeup invoked intense debate. I had long insisted I could not do it myself. Lolly said she could apply the makeup if someone else designed it. So, Chris made an appointment for me to sit down with Jesus, who, I was told, would teach me everything I needed to know about becoming a woman.

At 2 p.m. the following Saturday, I walked into a posh subterranean Soho makeup store looking for Jesus. The store, much larger than it appeared from the street, instantly overwhelmed me with its vast selection of run-of-the-mill cosmetics: base colors, eyeliners, lipstick, gloss, all the things you could easily find at Macy's.

I walked up to the counter and asked for Jesus.

"Jesus is in the back," the woman told me. "On the other side of those mirrors."

She pointed to a panel of floor-to-ceiling mirrors that seemed to divide the store in two. I walked around to the other side of the panels and could hardly believe what lay beyond. Since every wall was covered in mirrors, the much brighter light kept smashing into itself. Mirrored shelves held brightly colored make-up containers, stockings, and wigs.

"This must be where drag queens go when they die," I thought.

In the middle of the section, although it felt more like its own room, sat two barber chairs. I quietly walked around and looked at the various lip liners and eye shadow. The colors here were over the top, meant for the stage not for the street. That much I could tell.

"Excuse me," a voice said from behind me. "May I help you?"

"Yes, hi, I'm Randy Anderson," I turned around and extended my hand. "I'm supposed to meet with Jesus."

The small, very effeminate Latino man gingerly took my hand, pressing his palm to my fingers.

"Yes, I'm Jesus. How can I help you today?"

"Where are you from?" I asked, wanting to get a little personal before letting him work on my face.

"Let me guess. You think I'm Puerto Rican, don't you?"

"No," I said. "I didn't know. That's why I asked."

"Why does everyone assume I'm Puerto Rican? Does every Latino in this city have to be Puerto Rican?" He added an overdramatic sigh.

"No, that's not what I..."

"Ai yai yai! Papi! Then, why do you assume I'm from another country?"

Feeling totally stupid, I wanted desperately to steer away from the topic but couldn't seem to find my way.

"Because people don't name their kids Jesus in America."

"Dis is true, mijo. Americans don't like their kids to be called Jesus. Even the Latino kids get named Bill or Joe. It's so boring. Now, what can I do for you?"

Jesus didn't seem to know why I was there.

"Did you talk to my friend Chris about helping me with some drag makeup?" I asked, hoping I could jog his memory.

"No, papi. I didn't talk with nobody about you. But I can help you. Sit down. Tell me what you need."

Jesus drilled me with questions, first about my character, who I described to him; the purple dress, which I showed to him; and the wig, which I explained was still missing in action.

"Ai, papi, no! You cannot buy makeup until you know what wig you are going to wear." He frantically circled the room.

"We just haven't found the right one," I explained, not wanting to get into the sordid details of our arduous search. "We know we're looking for fire-engine red. But the really good ones cost a fortune, and the ones within our budget look cheap."

"Here," he said. "Close your eyes."

I did as he asked, prepared for him to put some eye shadow on me. Instead, I felt the tickle of long hairs on my neck and the subtle pressure of mesh close around my head.

"OK. Open your eyes."

I winced briefly at the sudden influx of light piercing my corneas, but as my focus sharpened, I saw the most amazingly beautiful, bright-red cascade falling off my head. This was the perfect wig.

"How much is this?" I asked with an overwhelming directness.

"I guess you like it!" Jesus said. "I give it to you for 200."

"Done!" I said without hesitating. "Now, can you design something to work with this wig?"

"You bet your little white ass I can."

Jesus pulled out little makeup containers by the fistful. Four hours and a whopping $400 later, I walked out of the store with a wig, a bag of more than two-dozen makeup containers, and a Polaroid of the final design. I had spent nearly 20 percent of our budget, and I braced myself for the inevitable lecture from my fellow producers.

"Rock-and-roll!" Lolly shouted as she placed the six-pack on one of the Odd Lot *Testing Average* TV trays now populating my apartment.

"Rock-and-roll!" I replied, grabbing one of the bottles. I had finished shaving 10 minutes earlier, and my face was perfectly smooth and dry—a blank canvas for Lolly to work her color magic.

The makeup ritual for *Theodora, She Bitch of Byzantium*, had become my favorite weekend activity. We started with the base. For 10 to 15 minutes, Lolly pressed a thick pancake base into my every pore to hide any semblance of a five o'clock shadow and even out my skin tone. Next, she would work from top to bottom. Penciling over my naturally sparse eyebrows took only a few minutes. Then, she'd spend a good 20 minutes on each eye—applying fake lashes, eyeliner, and eye shadow and pressing glitter onto the shadow.

For the next half-hour, she'd sculpt my cheekbones with highlights and lowlights and brighten them with blush so they'd pop. She'd do a little ladylike chin-thinning, then add the finishing touch: blazing red lips with red glitter thrown on top. Lolly had the whole routine down to 90 minutes—just enough time for us to finish the whole six-pack before heading down to the theater.

We packed our many costumes and props and headed to the train. Making downtown theater in New York demands a lot of schlepping—schlepping of sets, schlepping of costumes, schlepping of makeup, schlepping of props. Cars are expensive to own, rent, or hire, so for the off-off artists, schlepping is almost always the only option. But we didn't care. We were young, fit, and slightly buzzed. We would carry any amount of weight to make a show happen.

Sure, we'd get some funny looks on the train. The makeup was over the top, and without the wig, I looked even more bizarre. Plus, during the 30-minute ride to the East Village, Lolly would apply my nails.

Theodora had talons like a bird of prey. We had tried the press-on variety in rehearsal, but with all the people-grabbing and constant costume changes, we needed something more permanent. Nothing kills the image of a fearsome raptor faster than a claw springing off. So, everyone on the downtown C train got a weekly whiff of nail glue from 110th Street all the way to our West Fourth Street transfer.

For Lolly and I, the show had already started. We were rocking-and-rolling all the way downtown. After we got off the F train on Second Avenue, we stopped at the Mars bar on the corner. The Mars bar is a tiny dive frequented by men with bellies and beards—and not too many drag queens. But it's the East Village. The bartender didn't flinch when I ordered two shots of tequila and a couple of Buds.

Our earlier buzz had dissipated somewhere between Times Square and Washington Square, and we had at least 20 minutes before we needed to be at the theater. The drinks arrived. We toasted, threw back our shots, and settled into the barstools to sip our beers.

We hadn't always drunk so heavily before the show. It sort of crept up on us. For the first few weeks, we drank coffee and warmed up our articulators. Then, beers crept in during makeup time. And now, here we were, chasing shots of tequila with Budweisers an hour before curtain.

"Do you have any gum?" Lolly asked.

"Of course. A smoker's gotta carry gum."

"Good, 'cause this tequila's gonna make my breath stink, and I don't want any lectures from The Girls," said Lolly, digging through my jacket pocket for my Winterfresh.

"Nobody's gonna lecture you."

"I don't know, Randy. I don't think they like me very much."

This didn't alarm me, as I knew all about Lolly's strong personality.

"That's not true. I'm sure The Girls like you."

"Oh, I don't care if they like me. I just don't want a fucking lecture." She polished off her beer. "Are you ready?"

"Rock-and-roll!" I placed my empty on the bar.

We arrived at the theater just as the last show was clearing out and got into costume. The building was buzzing. At the KGB bar, folks leaving the 8 o'clock shows mingled with the patrons waiting for the 10:30 shows. A logjam of drunken commuters clogged the narrow staircase linking the two theaters and the bar. It was Saturday night at 85 East Fourth Street, and everyone was feeling good.

The pre-show music blared into the theater as people found their seats. We almost always came close to a sellout, thanks to curious acquaintances and those lured in at the last minute by the edgy title and the $9.99 ticket price.

By the time the show starts, the very vocal audience is primed for entertainment. The lights go down, voices quiet, and bodies settle. We fly through the first act seamlessly. Lolly, who plays Theodora's psychic advisor Fata Morgana, and I swap a few knowing glances during the first act. Clearly, we aren't the only ones who took the rock-and-roll direction to mean "get loaded backstage." Easily half the cast is buzzing. The performances become louder...faster...and funnier. Not the best diction, mind you, but louder...faster...and funnier. We are sailing through the show. The audience is having a great time. The performers are having a great time, and everything seems to be on target.

In the middle of the third act, as I finish a speech that precedes the entrance of Fata Morgana, I find myself alone in a pool of silence. Lolly isn't coming on stage. I repeat my line louder so she'll hear me. No entrance. I pause, look at the audience, and begin to disparage my trusted advisor. Then, we hear a loud thud against the stage-left door. Everyone watches as the doorknob turns back and forth quickly, as if someone were attempting to break in. But the door isn't locked. Muffled sounds fill the theater. I walk over and place my hand on the knob.

"Who could this be?" I say to the audience, pulling the door open. And there, hanging on the knob, is Lolly, being dragged on the floor by the opening door.

"Theodora!" she says, springing to her feet. "The fucking door's broke."

I walk back to center stage to continue the scene, but Lolly lunges toward me and reaches for my shoulders. I step back, as any lady would when someone is lunging toward her, and Lolly spills flat on her face. Her costume now twisting, I fear her tits might also make an unexpected entrance. Then, I notice the folks in the front row. Those brave few, whose feet are mere inches from Lolly's logrolling body, are waving their hands in front of their noses.

"She's drunk!" one of them says, causing an eruption of hysterical laughter.

"Fata, have you been drinking?" I ask, still in character.

"You bet your twat I have," she replies, gathering her faculties enough to stand.

Then, the smell hits me. It was as if she'd gargled Jack Daniels and rinsed out with Stoli. Only later did I learn that the cast members who didn't appear in Act Two had made a trip down to the KGB bar for several shots before Act Three.

Thankfully, our scene consists of only five lines followed by Fata dying on stage. Lolly somehow manages to spit out her lines and die. Relieved, I await the next entrance. Big Rob, playing my husband Justinian, stumbles on and slurs something about feathers. And the parade of drunks continues. They come on, do their little scene, die loudly, and lie in peace.

By the time the whole cast has assembled around my feet in a pile of corpses, the theater smells like a fermentation plant. I complete my last monologue, stab myself, and end the show in a heap on the floor. The cast's drunkenness is not lost on the audience, but they embrace the rock-and-roll spirit and leap to their feet in thunderous applause. As if running for office, Lolly launches into the audience and shakes the hands of each and every audience member. It couldn't have been more successful.

After the show, a furious Chris burst into the dressing room. We quickly attempted to hide our open containers as if we were 17-year-olds boozing in the garage.

"What the fuck are you guys thinking?" he whisper-shouted.

"I may have overdone it during Act Two," Lolly admitted sheepishly.

"Me too!" said her obvious accomplice, Big Rob.

"A little bit?" I asked with a smile "Your costume was on sideways. You can't walk straight."

The room burst into laughter.

"It's not funny!" Chris said. "That show totally sucked."

"Right," Lolly countered. "That's why they gave us a standing ovation."

"Come on, Chris," I said. "They had a good time."

"That's not the show I directed."

"You said this show was rock-and-roll!" said Lolly, exposing her open beer bottle from under her wig and brazenly taking a swig.

"I didn't mean get loaded. That's disrespectful to your audience and to the stage."

His lecture made us feel like bad kids, and we loved it. We relished our bad behavior because we felt like rock stars, and rock stars behave badly. We contemplated throwing chairs down the stairwell but decided in the end that we weren't that hard core. We weren't heavy metal. Just good, old-fashioned rock-and-roll.

SO FUCKING WHAT

The evening was called *SFW*, which are Stephanie's initials, but for the purpose of the show, they stood for *So Fucking What*. It was a punk-rock-meets-sexy-piano-girl-in-a-cabaret-setting kind of evening. Stephanie had been working on her album in the Bronx and had a slew of new songs ready to perform.

We booked the cabaret space above Rose's Turn, a piano bar on Christopher Street in the West Village, and were going to keep it simple—just Stephanie on the piano with Lolly and Bobby singing back-up on a few songs.

We rehearsed in Stephanie's Bronx apartment, where her boyfriend, Jared, had a recording studio. Several times a week, we took the 1 train to the end of the line, then walked up 240 steps to her building at the top of the hill. I'd met Jared a few times. One-hundred-percent rapper, he used street language and had a street attitude. Their apartment décor consisted of expensive leather couches, half-burnt blunts, an aggressive pit-bull, and enough electronic equipment to launch the space shuttle. Walking into their world was like walking into a movie.

"Sometimes, his friends will come over to help us record, and I'll have to tell them to leave their guns in the kitchen," Stephanie told us one day. "I don't sing as well when there are guns in the studio. I can't relax or something."

The idea that someone could, at any moment, enter the apartment with a gun simultaneously thrilled and terrified me.

The show sounded great, and Jared decided to arrange a live recording, which I foolishly green-lighted. He pulled me out of rehearsal one evening to discuss it.

"So Randy," he began. "I'm gonna need some cash to get some things for this recording."

"What do you mean? I thought you already had all the equipment."

The more I produced, the more I got used to people asking for money. It's part of the job. But this was the first time someone without a budget had asked me for money—not to mention someone who was probably packing heat.

"I ain't hauling it all down there. Shit's too big. I have to get me some portable..." Everything I hear after this is blah-blah-blah-technical-technical-blah-blah.

"I don't know what to tell you. I wasn't anticipating any recording costs. We've got a $300 budget for this show, and we already spent that on the space and postcards."

"Well, you're gonna have to find me some money because I need cable and...blah-blah-technical-technical-blah-blah."

Still very calm, he was inching closer to me, and while he wasn't as tall as I, he was much wider and, gun or not, I was certain he could fuck my shit up pretty quick.

"Look," I said. "If you can't record the show, you can't record it. I don't have any more money to spend on this project."

Jared backed up, looked away for a moment, and then stepped in even closer.

"Listen up, Randy. Stephanie really wants me to record the show. I'm donatin' my time and my expertise to this show. And now you're expectin' me to give my money, too? That's fucked up."

It might have been my overactive imagination, but I thought I heard the dog in the other room sharpening his teeth against the floorboards.

"Jared, I don't know what to tell you. I'm producing the show, not the recording. That's your department. If you can't get all the equipment you need down there, I guess you can't record the show."

"Is that the way it's going to be?" he asked.

I paused. And then, I pulled the courage that hides behind my bellybutton up through my throat.

"No, that's the way it is, and the way it's always been. Now, if you'll excuse me, I've got to get back to rehearsal."

I turned my back and left the room, imagining I could hear the sound of a gun hammer being pulled back. That was the last time Jared and I spoke about money.

Really finding my stride as a producer, I was organized, efficient, and unemotional—three essential characteristics for the job.

Unfortunately, these are not the most ideal characteristics for a relationship.

One night after rehearsal, I headed down to C.J.'s place for take-out and some desperately needed sleep.

"Randy, I want to talk to you," he said, as we sat cross-legged on his living room floor, laying out our Indian food.

"OK, let's talk!" I dipped my naan into curry sauce.

"I need us to be more involved in each other's lives." My spine straightened as I realized the nature of the talk. "I mean, I was at G last night, and everyone was asking me where you were. I had to tell them you were at home. Sleeping!"

"I was tired. I didn't feel like going out. Besides, I hate G." Pretentious boy bars are not my thing.

"Well, that's where my friends like to go," C.J. replied defensively.

"It's pretentious, C.J.!"

"I know, but Randy, we're 24, and you're going to sleep at 9 o'clock on a Saturday night," he said, as if it were a crime.

"I'm sorry, but I was tired. I've been working on this show for the past two weeks—which means I go to sleep at two and wake up at seven. Saturday is my night off. I'm tired, so I sleep."

I didn't understand why he was getting so bent out of shape when I just didn't want to go drinking that night. Even I gave my liver a break every now and then.

"You're always working on shows."

"Well, that's what I like to do."

"You're taking this wrong. This isn't… what I'm trying to communicate to you is…that I need more access to you. You need to let me in more."

"What do you mean? I don't know what you mean." I studied his body language for signs of distancing, which I could detect in every appendage.

"I mean, you're not letting me into your life. I need someone who understands me. I mean…"

His head dropped down, almost as if he were looking for clarity in the saag panir.

"I mean, you spend all this time with your theater company, which is great, and I'm bragging to all my friends about what you're doing, but when I bring them to the shows…"

He paused. I knew what he was about to say. While he's never said it, I've always suspected.

"They're not good. Your shows are bad… and it's embarrassing. I'm embarrassed to bring my friends to your shows."

I'd always felt he was less than impressed with my work, but embarrassed? That felt too harsh. While I didn't care what his friends thought of me, *he* did. Of course, he cared. They were his friends. The conversation continued, but I was no longer present. My walls were already 10 feet high and three feet thick. He talked about my unwillingness to bring him into my creative process and his desire to participate more in the "Chelsea scene," even though he'd tell me he didn't like it. Communication, openness, his need to be understood—all were put on the table, all the typical relationship issues that, at this point in my life, didn't really interest me. I made a good show of listening and responding, but I couldn't get beyond the fact that my plays embarrassed him. I took great offence to that. And the fucker didn't even have the decency to bring me flowers.

"Well, I guess that's it then," I said as I stood up.

"What's *it*?" C.J. replied, following me up.

"I guess we're done." I stepped over the food on the floor, took a garbage bag from the kitchen, and headed to the bedroom.

"What are you doing?" asked C.J., following me.

"I'm getting my stuff and going home. I don't want to be an embarrassment to you." I filled the bag with socks and underwear.

"That's not what I meant, Randy, and you know it. I didn't... You're not an embarrassment. Come on, let's talk about this."

"I don't think there's anything else to talk about. You've pretty much said it all." I was surprised at the amount of clothing I had transported to his apartment.

"So you're going to leave. Just like that?"

"Yes."

I was amazingly calm. It was as if we were engaged in a business transaction. And despite his lame protestations to the contrary, I knew this was what he wanted.

"It's clear this is not working. Good-bye, C.J."

I opened the door. He stepped in to give me a hug, and I let the bag fall to the floor and embraced him. It was neat and clean and devoid of feelings.

"Can I still come to the show next week?"

"Of course, you can. And bring some friends. Stephanie's good. You won't be embarrassed."

I turned around, walked down the hall of his building, and stepped out onto the street. I'm sure this scene plays out hundreds of times a week in New York City. A man or woman, holding a bag of belongings, steps out onto the street fresh from a breakup. I paused on the West Village stoop and contemplated the unoriginality of my situation—and how strange and original it felt to me. I dragged the garbage bag to Eighth Avenue and hailed a cab.

When I got home, Lolly and Bobby were watching a movie. I announced C.J. and I had broken up, and they immediately jumped from the sofa and followed me into my bedroom, where I began unpacking my Hefty bag. They drilled me with a million questions and offered words of comfort, most of which I didn't want. As far as I was concerned, the less fuss, the better. We had shows to work on, flyers to make, and grant proposals to write. It seemed a terrible waste of energy to wax on about the end of my 11-month relationship. I did what I was best at: suppress and press on.

On the night of the show, I arrived at Rose's Turn early. We were the first act, and I wanted to set up the stage. Our contract had strictly forbidden any kind of set—only the piano and mike stands were allowed. So, when I told the manager I wanted to get in a half-hour early, she looked at me suspiciously. I finally convinced her I wasn't going to break any rules and got into the space to...well...break the rules by hanging some paintings. We wanted to create a comfortable feeling on stage, so we took some of Stephanie's personal paintings and hung them from the grid with fishing line. The effect was magical—floating paintings around a baby grand.

The bartender arrived and began setting up. I ordered a Corona and hovered around, looking for anyone who needed help. Lolly and Bobby were going over their music in the dressing room. When Stephanie and Jared showed up, I polished off my Corona and went out to help them load in the recording equipment.

Jared, wanting nothing to do with me, had recruited a friend to help him, so I followed Stephanie back into the theater. I bought another Corona on my way past the bar and joined the crew in the dressing room, which was too small for four people. So, I went back out into the house and saw our technician. Eager to have something to do, I immediately went over the light cues with him. Since there were only three cues repeated over and over, this took only five minutes. We still had more than a half-hour before people would start arriving, and I was listless. I ordered another Corona and sat in the back of the audience watching Jared and his friend construct their recording table.

I was terribly nervous about this show and wanted desperately to be doing something. Yet I had no reason to be so antsy. I wasn't performing, we had plenty of reservations, and we were sure to make back our tiny investment. But still, my stomach fluttered like mad. I finished my beer and headed out to the street for a cigarette.

The sun had gone down, and the city was cast in twilight. The West Village streets were beginning to fill with people looking at dinner menus and meeting friends in front of bars. I walked to the corner of Seventh Avenue and looked down to the Actor's Playhouse, the site of my New York debut. Looking north, I could see the apartment C.J. lived in when I first met him. He had since moved to a quieter West Village street, away from the nightlife and his roommate. And then I realized why I was so nervous. I lit a fresh cigarette with the butt of the one I just smoked and walked back to the entrance of Rose's Turn.

The manager was outside smoking a cigarette and I joined her. "You expecting a big house?" she asked

"About 40 people...which means 30 will show up."

"Thirty's pretty good," she said. "We can open the house whenever you want."

"Let's do it."

I stamped out my butt in the sand-filled bucket and headed upstairs. I got another beer on my way backstage and stepped over a nest of cables Jared had created on stage left.

"Are you gonna move those?" I asked, not breaking my stride.

"To the side a little," Jared replied without looking up. "We got no place else to put them."

"As long as nobody can trip on them." I poked my head into the dressing room. "We're opening the house, gang. Break a leg!"

Stephanie, Bobby, and Lolly were laughing and singing. They all looked pretty relaxed. Stephanie seemed a little jumpy, but she'd calm down after the first song. The house music came on—which was actually House music, thanks to Jared—and I stood by the door to greet guests as they entered. I'd been talking up Stephanie for months, so a lot of my friends were curious to see what all the fuss was about. Since I knew almost everyone, the greetings part was easy.

Then, C.J. turned the corner. I saw him before he saw me, and I turned and walked toward the booth, pretending I had something to tell the technician.

"You want a beer?" I asked him, hoping he'd say no.

"That'd be great! Get me a Bud."

Not the answer I was looking for, but going to the bar would give me something to do. And I could use another beer anyway. C.J. spotted me on my way back from the bar.

"Randy, hey!" he said standing up.

"C.J., I'm glad you made it. I'd give you a proper greeting but..." I held up the drinks in my hand.

"You better slow down. The night is young."

"One of these is for the technician."

"I know. It was a joke."

"I know. Um, I better get this to him. We're going to start soon. See you downstairs at the bar after?" I asked, as I awkwardly stepped through the mess of people and chairs.

"Um, sure, OK," he replied.

It was forced. He had no intention of staying after, and now he was going to feel obligated. I thought about going back and telling him I wouldn't be downstairs later after all, that I had an appointment I'd forgotten. But by the time I dropped off the Bud, C.J. was already in deep conversation with the people at his table. I stood around uncomfortably until the lights went down and the show began.

For the next hour, Stephanie sang her heart out and hammered on that baby grand. Lolly and Bobby ooh-ed and aah-ed in the background, and everyone seemed to be into the music. After the curtain call, Stephanie invited everyone to join us downstairs, and I quickly cleared the three empty beer bottles I had downed during the show and stumbled downstairs to secure a section for our party.

I commandeered a section at the back of the bar by laying my body across four chairs, but our party was already filling the space themselves. So, I got up, chatted briefly with some guests and, feeling very good about the evening, went to get another drink at the bar, where I noticed one of C.J.'s snobby friends standing next to me.

"That was a good show," he said. "How do you know her?"

I really didn't want to engage in a conversation with him. This particularly pretentious, obnoxious friend had accused me of trying to hit on him, confusing an animated conversation with a sexual advance.

"Glad you liked it. From college. Can I have Corona please?" I quickly turned my back to him in search of a friendly face. When I looked back to the bar, I saw the bartender pour my Corona into a plastic cup.

"You don't have to do that. I can drink it from the bottle."

"Yes I do, and no you can't," the bartender replied.

I was oddly amused and confused by the meaning of this. I brushed it off and started toward our group only to be intercepted by C.J.

"Hey, Randy, only one drink this time? Can I get that proper greeting now?" He smiled, holding his arms open.

"How can you be so happy?" I asked, ignoring the invitation to hug.

"I'm happy to see you. I'm proud of you. I miss you." The kind words took me off guard. "I mean, our breaking up was for the best, but I'm glad we can still be friends."

I listened intently as I drank my beer, which because of that plastic cup poured into my gullet much faster. While I was the one who left, I had suspected he wanted out and now that suspicion was confirmed.

"I don't want to be your friend, C.J. I want to be your boyfriend." I tried to keep my voice lower than the volume of the room.

"Randy," he started, and I knew by his tone where he was going. "I cried for hours after you left.

Hours. But we're not...it wasn't working." His friend had retrieved his drink and joined us.

"Why not?" My volume increased. "I LOVE YOU! Doesn't that count for something? Do you love me or not?"

C.J.'s friend tried to change the subject as Stephanie walked by.

"Good job!" he said. And Stephanie turned to me.

"Are you OK?" she asked.

"I'm fine," I replied, not taking my eyes off C.J.

"So, what did you think of the show?"

"I'm in the middle of something right now," I said, trying to remain calm. "Can we talk about it later?"

"No," she insisted. "Tell me now."

I unlocked my gaze on C.J. and looked directly at Stephanie.

"It wasn't my favorite. You could have done better. Now, please excuse me."

Stephanie turned and walked away taking C.J.'s friend with her.

"Randy," C.J. said. "You've got to calm down."

"Why should I calm down? You broke my heart, C.J.!"

"You broke up with *me!*"

"Only because that's what you wanted me to do. But I love you. Don't you see that? I FUCKING LOVE YOU!"

My head was spinning. I was flushed and had lost control of my volume. People were watching us as if we were some after-show.

"I loved you, too, Randy, but not anymore."

"Right. Because I embarrass you."

"Well, you're embarrassing me now, that's for sure."

I didn't know how to respond. I realized I was embarrassing him. And I also realized I was embarrassing myself, but I was so mad and so heartbroken, I didn't care.

"I HATE YOU FOR BREAKING MY HEART!"

And I emptied the rest of my beer right in his face. We stood there in silence, both of us in shock over what had just happened—his face soaked and my face, for the moment, dry.

Suddenly, two hands on my back began pushing me toward the door. I could see, from my periphery, everyone in the bar was staring at me, but I kept my gaze forward. I let the hands push me all the way to the door, which the bouncer gladly opened. By the time we got into the street, tears were sliding off my chin. As my hands reached up to wipe them away, I broke into a full sob. Bobby threw his arms around me and guided me down the street toward the subway.

"OK, buddy, we're going to take you home," he said, his voice soft and comforting. "It's OK. You're going to be OK. Oh my God, you're so drunk!" He was having some difficulty steering me in a straight line. "I'm glad you're finally letting something out. I was beginning to wonder if you were human."

"I love him, Bobby. I love him," was all I could say between the sobs.

I cannot remember a time in my life when I cried that hard. Twenty-four years old, and I had yet to experience a significant loss. And any loss I had suffered, I'd suppressed to the point of not experiencing it. We got to the subway platform and sat on the bench. My wails of emotional torment continued. Overdramatic cries emanated from my gut and poured out relentless tears. I was still embarrassing myself, but Bobby didn't mind. With his arm over my shoulders, he made sure everyone knew I was in good hands.

A passing woman handed Bobby a fistful of tissues. Obviously concerned, she was cautious not to get too close to my convulsing. The train ride home was long and painful. And once there, I climbed right into bed. Finally alone, I could, for the first time, hear myself cry. The sound was absolutely terrifying...which made me feel more alone...which made me cry harder. This didn't stop until my body had felt enough and completely shut down for the night.

The days following were stark and difficult. Through an epic 48-hour hangover, I had a number of phone calls to make, apologies to issue, and forgiveness to beg for. In representing The Beggars Group that night, I had totally broken character in front of our patrons. But the people I called were very gracious. Everyone, it seemed, had been heartbroken and drunk before. And while they were just trying to be sympathetic and nice, it only served to make me feel sophomoric. And then I'd make another call. How could I be the only person who'd never been heartbroken? I longed to commiserate with a "fellow" teenager.

A week later, I quit my job. Not only was I helplessly lovesick, I had discovered I could see into C.J.'s office from our conference room—and my boss had binoculars. It just became too much to go into the office day after day. I couldn't bear to talk to people and do the job. Instead, I spent my days sitting in my room listening to Rufus Wainwright bang out my emotions on his piano. Inconsolable, I wandered the streets for exercise and smoked cigarettes for nourishment.

One day, before a Beggars Group meeting, Lolly found me sitting in the gutter outside the Hungarian Pastry Shop. She sat down next to me. "You look so pathetic sitting in the gutter like this."

"It's the perfect manifestation of how I feel."

"Oh!" She tenderly put her arm around me. "Well, are you going to come in and be a Beggar, or are you gonna stay out here and be a bum?"

"In a minute. I didn't realize you'd started."

"We haven't yet, but it'd be great if you were there when we did."

"Yeah, OK."

"We're not going to keep doing this without you, Randy. I realize you're depressed and all, but you have to keep moving forward. You've put too much work into this company to let it fall apart because of fucking C.J."

I liked the sound of her calling him that. It was childish but made me feel good.

"Did I tell you he hated *Testing Average*? He and his friends thought it was awful. He was embarrassed by it."

"So, he's a dick. So what? Didn't one of your co-workers describe it as one of her favorite theatrical experiences? Didn't she talk to you about it for weeks? Just because you were in love with the guy doesn't mean he knows jackshit about theater. And even if he did, who cares if he didn't like it? Lots of people are going to hate the work we do. And lots of others are going to love it. Now, if everyone starts coming out of our shows saying it was 'all right,' then we have a problem. But man, let's be bold! Like you, right now, sitting in this gutter. It's bold and dramatic. Lots of people are walking by thinking you're a real idiot."

"Yeah?"

"Yeah! But so fucking what, Randy. We've got to be true to ourselves. You have to be true to *you*. And making theater is what we're doing right now, so let's concentrate, stay focused, and just do that for now."

"So fucking what," I repeated, laughing a little.

"It's gonna take time for you to get over C.J., but don't let everything else get fucked-up in the process. Now come on, The Girls are waiting! Don't make me go in there and face them alone."

She stood up and offered her hand. Real life as metaphor: Here was Lolly, literally pulling me out of the gutter.

And that was the moment I decided to stop spending every waking moment on my failed relationship. I would take a full-time job at Blah-Blah Big Bank to resurrect my cash flow and spend the rest of my hours diligently focused on building this theater company and doing what I loved. Because I knew I loved making theater, and I knew I didn't love being sad.

"Have you talked to Stephanie?" Lolly asked.

"Not since the night of the show. She's not returning my calls. I'm pretty sure she hates me."

"Yeah, I'm pretty sure she does, too," Lolly agreed, as we walked toward the tantalizing aroma of coffee and baked goods.

I'd found my direction, and life had thrown some obstacles. But somehow, I managed to stay the course and continue refining my definition of success.

Part III
THE EXPATRIATES

X MARKS THE SPOT

Bobby dropped his cigarette butt between the rusted slats of the fire escape, and we watched it fall six stories to the ground. It was cold out here, but things were getting a little too hot inside. So, we were taking the fire escape at its word.

"Do you think it's safe to go back in?" Bobby asked.

"Probably not," I replied. "But I think we have no choice. Break's over."

I lifted the windowsill and rolled off the fire escape back into the studio. We'd rented a Chelsea studio to take publicity photos for *The Expatriates*, and so far, things weren't going so well.

The play itself was progressing nicely. As the head writer, I collected and compiled the submissions from the other five writers. And while no one had submitted much actual dialogue yet, we were throwing around a bounty of ideas. Collaborative writing is a tricky business, but I was doing my diplomatic best to ensure everyone's ideas were heard and to keep things moving forward.

The photo-shoot idea came from The Girls, who were fascinated with the expatriates' fascination with Dadaism. So, we decided to do a Dada-inspired photo shoot with Dorothy Parker, Zelda Fitzgerald, Sara Murphy, and a little-known composer named George Antheil.

Lolly, our fearless director, had been reading Antheil's autobiography and insisted I play the part of George. I hesitated at first. I wasn't sure the character fit into the play, and I didn't want to act in the show. With my dual roles as producer and head writer, the last thing I wanted was to wear another hat. But the very persuasive Lolly knew how to get me excited about something. The night before the photo shoot, after two hours of gushing about George Antheil's life, she threw out an image that excited my imagination and my interest.

"So, at one point, when he's 22 or 23, he's performing the second of two modern-music concerts in Germany," she started.

"The night before, there had been a riot. The Germans, it turns out, didn't love this new 'modern' music. That, and the fact it was the '20s, and they were all still pissed about losing the war. So, on the second night, he walks out on stage. The audience claps politely. George then orders all the attendants to close and lock all the exits. Can you believe that? You could never do that today. He tells the audience he will not tolerate another riot and that he has brought a gun to ensure everyone behaves. And he pulls a gun out of his tuxedo and places it on the piano! An American pulling a fucking gun out on a bunch of Germans in the '20s. I mean, if he were French, he'd be dead in a second.

"Anyway, he puts this gun on the piano and says, 'Anyone who misbehaves will be shot.' Silence. Then, he sits down and plays his full concert without a peep. How fucking cool was this guy? Now, I got this from his autobiography, which I'm pretty sure he half made up, but who cares, right? It's a great story."

She looked at me, waiting for a reaction. How could I say "no" to playing a guy like *that*? It's like saying "no" to playing James Bond. So, I arrived at the photo shoot, dressed in black pants, a white shirt, and a secondhand tuxedo jacket two sizes too big. Not the most fashionable but perfect for concealing a gun.

The photographer arrived with a camera that looked at least 50 years old.

"Wow, we're really going for period here, aren't we?" I joked.

"It's actually the same kind of camera that took pictures on the moon," said Deborah, correcting me.

"I hope the quality's better," Bobby said. "Those moon pictures are kind of fuzzy."

"We're working with much better light," said the photographer, as she kicked open the legs of her tripod.

I wasn't sure about that. The light is pretty good on the moon, the bright side of it anyway.

The trouble started when we began putting on our makeup.

The Expatriates didn't take place in a real time. We were not in Paris, 1927. Our play took place in a purgatorial realm where we could easily jump through time and hit all the juicy moments of our characters' lives. To set this up, we were going to exhume these people, quite literally, from a coffin on stage.

Our makeup needed to be ghost-like. Not bloody and decayed like a zombie, but more like a ghoul—a ghost with weight. We'd discovered that a light dusting of white on our faces created a nice image of a spirit...dead without being too monster-ish.

Once we determined the exact intensity, everyone got behind the white dusting, but we agreed less about the eyes. Sunken eyes with the white dusting would be too monster-like, so we needed to find a different direction. Lolly wanted everyone to have what she called "Big Eyes." She kept walking around the room encouraging us to lay the eyeliner on thicker. Since I didn't fully understand, I asked Lolly to apply my makeup for me, and she jumped at the opportunity.

"You guys," she said as I looked up, "the eyes need to really pop!"

I could see her widening her own eyes as she stared into mine, working the pencil back and forth across my lower lid.

"You're entering this world for a second time. You know you've been dead for however long, and now you're walking back into the world of the living, and there's all this life around you to absorb. It's like your eyes are swollen from taking in the richness of everything. I want to see the word 'AWAKE' in your eyes.

You're awake!" She leaned back to take in my whole face. "See! Like this."

The Girls craned their necks to look.

"That's too much!" Andrea said. "We don't want to look like clowns."

Andrea had just lobbed a Molotov cocktail into the center of the room. The conversation exploded into a heated argument about the subtle differences between clowns and Dada.

Not knowing much about either, I carefully extracted myself, dragging Bobby outside for a smoke with me. I was, at that moment, an actor, not the producer, and I was going to do what my director told me.

I guess I could have predicted this argument. Everyone had so many roles to play, so much invested, and such varied ideas about the project that without a tremendous ability to yield, fights were inevitable. As we climbed onto the fire escape, voices were amplifying and the name-calling began.

When we returned, everyone was quietly applying makeup and double-checking their clothes.

"Are we almost ready to start shooting?" I asked hopefully.

"I'm ready," said the photographer, turning on her light tester.

"I'm just about ready, too!" said Deborah, in her best Zelda Fitzgerald voice.

We all did a double-take. Not only had she painted on the thick black eyeliner as Lolly had instructed, she also drew black eyelashes that radiated out from the bottom of her eyes.

"Now that's what I'm talking about!" Lolly said, clapping. "That looks awesome!"

She was right. It *did* look awesome. It conveyed AWAKE very clearly. Andrea, as Dorothy Parker, and Kathy, as Sara Murphy, had also done a great job of abstracting not just their eyes but their lips as well. The four of us looked otherworldly, familiar, and interesting.

"This is gonna be awesome!" said Bobby, as Lolly began arranging us on the platform.

We assumed angular positions, held them for a while, and then moved to the next pose. As the camera flashed, Lolly would call out directions.

"Look here! Big Eyes!"

"Look there! Big Eyes!"

"Randy, look left, Big Eyes! Kathy, look up, Big Eyes!"

After we posed and made Big Eyes for a solid 20 minutes, Lolly abruptly stopped the action and walked over to me, opening an eyeliner pencil.

"We're missing something."

When she approached, I instinctively opened my eyes and looked up, but she tilted my head down and turned my face to the side and drew what felt like two lines on my cheek. "There we go!" she said out loud, as she guided my head to turn the other way and drew two lines on my other cheek.

"What are you doing?" Deborah gasped.

"I'm putting Xs on your cheeks," Lolly replied.

The Girls responded in a chorus of disapproval, each one talking louder than the other.

"What for? That makes no logical sense?" Andrea managed to condense their rising discontent into a precision response.

"Who cares about logic? Do you think these people cared about logic? Do you think any of them were worried about logic? I mean, it's just an X. It's X marks the spot, X for Expatriates, X'd out of existence. Take your pick. It's the Dada X."

Lolly was on a roll. Her creative juices were flowing, and she wasn't backing down.

"But that's not what this play is about!" Kathy barked.

"Well, that's what this photo shoot is about," Lolly countered.

"But these pictures have to convey what the play is about. We can't just make shit up!" said Kathy.

"Why not?" Lolly asked. "George Antheil was never in a room with these people. Dorothy Parker wasn't buddy-buddy with the Murphys and Hemingway. We're making a lot of shit up. A lot of shit that's going to make for a great fucking play."

"Not if you're putting Xs on our faces!" Kathy said.

"No Kathy, *because* I'm putting Xs on your faces."

Lolly's tone demanded the conversation be over. As the only one who actually *had* Xs on his face, I felt it best not to get involved—either that, or I just don't like confrontation. Andrea, sensing this route was going nowhere, tried a different angle.

"Isn't 'decay' the theme we're working with here?" she asked.

"Yes," Lolly replied.

"The idea that as a fruit ripens, it gets more colorful?" Andrea continued.

"Yes."

"Sweeter-smelling?"

"Yes."

"Better-tasting?"

"Yes."

"And that this moment comes just prior to the fruit rotting? In fact, can it be said that the ripening is actually the beginning of the rotting process?"

"Yes."

We were all riveted, waiting for Lolly to say something more than "yes," as she'd been talking ad nauseam on the topic of decay for the past two weeks.

"And this is our allegorical approach to depicting this era and these people. They are living at the very sweetest moment in their lives and in the country. The brightest, most colorful seconds before they descend into putrid-smelling decay and eventual death."

Andrea had done it! Her elegant wording got that entire room to understand the concept for the very first time.

"Yes," Lolly said simply.

"Well, then why are you putting Xs on our faces?" Andrea asked.

"Because I don't have any rotten fruit," Lolly said flatly.

"Randy!" Andrea cried, turning toward me. "Say something."

I didn't know how to help the situation. I really didn't give a shit about the Xs. I just wanted to take some pictures. I was the model, not the artist. I looked over at Bobby to see if he might have an objective opinion, but he was too busy containing his laughter over the rotten fruit jab. The room fell into a silence for a moment.

"Look, you guys, I've already got a lot of shots," our photographer offered. "I'm sure we have more than enough to work with. I only have one roll left anyway. Why don't we call it a day?"

"That sounds like a great idea," Andrea said, as Kathy and Deborah followed her into the kitchen and began removing their makeup.

"Well, let's at least take a few with the X-faced George Antheil," Lolly said.

She sat me on a stool, gave me a stack of papers, and told me to start throwing them into the air while looking at the camera—which is how we used the last roll of film.

"What are these mysterious Xs on his face?" people would later ask. "What do they mean?"

We didn't know, but when we got the proofs back, we knew we'd have to start looking for an answer. Because the shots of this man with Xs on his face, levitating paper, were dynamite.

FIRE-FOOD

"HOW DARE YOU!" I screamed as I stood, launching the wheeled executive chair out from under me. "I specifically asked you what this meeting was about, and you told me it was about work. Work! Not feelings. Do you remember that? I told you if this was about your feelings, I wasn't available."

My voice echoed through the maze of cubicles and conference rooms on the 43rd floor of the Investment Bank where The Girls worked as night secretaries.

It was past 10 p.m., and the bankers were gone. I discovered I could be a different person in this environment. We held a lot of our meetings in the conference rooms of Fortune 500 companies. It was a million-dollar set for a thousand-dollar theater company. Here, I could channel my Wall Street callousness. Here, we did most of our photocopying and supply-shopping. It's not stealing, we told ourselves. It's an "involuntary corporate donation."

Kathy finally spoke up.

"I knew you wouldn't come if I told you what this was about."

"Of course, you did. You knew because I told you. And you lied to me anyway. Shame on you."

"Will you just listen to us?"

"I've sat here for 20 minutes listening to you. You're feeling vulnerable. You're feeling abused by Lolly. You're feeling like the show has moved in the wrong direction. I hear you. But guess what? I'm tired. I'm anxious. I'm mad at Lolly. The show never moves in the direction you think it's going to—and that, my friends, is called making theater. Put your fucking feelings away. We open in two days. We got shit to do. We'll talk about feelings after we open."

The room fell silent, and then just to emphasize the obvious, I slammed my fists on the table. "I am *furious* with you!"

Kathy burst into tears and ran out of the room. Andrea and Deborah followed, shooting hateful glances at me on their way out. Bobby rolled my chair into the back of my knees. I sat and took a breath.

"Dude," Lolly said. We sat in silence for another minute. I wondered if Lolly was going to ask me why I was mad at her, but she didn't. That would be a feelings talk, and we were on the same page about saving that shit for a different day.

"That was awesome," she said finally. And she burst into laughter.

A smile cracked the corners of my mouth. As angry as I was, I felt a small sense of satisfaction. The Girls had lured us down there under false pretenses. Bobby tried to calm Lolly down with a disapproving look. But she'd been counting on this for a while, and she was going to enjoy it.

Despite her satisfaction, we couldn't mask the fact we had a disaster on our hands. The company's morale had been in a freefall since the beginning of the summer. Tempers had flared up on multiple occasions. Up until this moment, I'd managed to maintain my cool. While bullets flew around me, I'd kept my head down and charged forward, guiding the group toward the finish line.

But now, overcome by a cocktail of exhaustion, determination, and anxiety, I'd lost my composure. Feeling drained, confused, and somehow excited, I looked at Lolly on my left, snickering into her hands, and Bobby on my right, shaking his head in total disapproval. They looked like the devil and the angel, sitting on each of my shoulders, whispering their temptations into my ear.

The fact that Bobby was playing the part of the angel forced me to seriously contemplate the severity of my behavior. The Girls weren't wrong to feel the way they did. They just had really bad timing—bad emotional timing. If they had come to me a few weeks earlier…

"You know…" Bobby said, interrupting my thoughts. "They've been trying to talk to you about this for months."

Fuck! It was true. I knew it was true. I was dismissing it as insecure nonsense, hoping it would go away. I never thought insecure nonsense could grow into anger, then hatred, then tears. And I remember thinking my ability to be empathetic was shockingly poor. Not that I wanted to do anything about it. But I recognized it.

Of the many minor dysfunctions I wasn't addressing, I had ignored the Lolly-versus-Girls problem for far too long. And it wasn't just The Girls. The entire cast disliked Lolly as a director. But haven't we all had directors we didn't like? I didn't understand what was burning them up so much. Lolly was available to talk anytime. Why didn't they sit down over a cup of coffee and discuss it? Were their differences so drastic?

As a writing team, The Girls and I were highly functional. We had set up a series of deadlines, and we all met them. We were extremely supportive of each other's efforts, knowing this was the first time many had written dialogue. Our process had been exciting, fulfilling, and largely un-dramatic, and that made the current situation even more perplexing. I started mining my memory to see how far back this problem went.

We'd completed a decent working script a week before rehearsals began and were proud of our accomplishment. Lolly affirmed its merit but had very clear ideas about the visual texture and tone of the piece. After our first reading, I could tell the script was too pedestrian for her vision.

In our play, Zelda Fitzgerald has written what the other characters recognize as a superior book. Is it a novel or a manifesto? Nobody can put a finger on it, but clearly they feel threatened by it. Right from the start, Ernest Hemingway takes shots at Zelda with his rifle, Dorothy Parker verbally assaults her, and her loving husband F. Scott tries his drunken best to put her back in her womanly place. But Zelda just frolics through the play, immune to their attacks because she knows she'll get the last laugh.

As we see what she has written, everything starts to fall apart. Her book is the story of their lives, told in heartbreaking detail.

When the book opens (which literally happens on stage), we are treated to snapshots, everything from romantic first meetings and decadent soirees, to adulterous affairs and miserable bouts with depression. Zelda captures their lives, not in their entirety, but at the ripest moments, those moments of raw beauty and unstoppable, horrible decay.

"This is a great base," Lolly began at the top of our first rehearsal. "I want to add a few things."

We listened with eager ears, excited for feedback from a new mind.

"First," she continued, "I'm going to add a character." This certainly wasn't the feedback we had hoped for, but we listened. "This character won't be a real person per se...rather more of a symbolic, or I should say allegoric, representation..."

"What is this person's name?" I asked, attempting to get her to the point. She could have been talking about Pablo Picasso, Gerald Murphy, or, God forbid, Ezra Pound. Lolly paused and then answered quickly.

"Fire-Food. The character is called Fire-Food."

The way she said it almost made us think we knew someone named Fire-Food—as if a quick search of our minds would reveal memories of classmates named Fire-Food, an uncle we affectionately called Fire-Food, or Fire-Food, a first love. The tactic was brilliant. We were all so disarmed by her nonchalance, we sat in silence, unable to question the moniker's legitimacy for fear of offending the one person in the room who had a cousin named Fire-Food.

"You'll see. She's going to add ritual and mystery to the show."

We had no doubt a character named Fire-Food would add mystery to the show. I quickly decided to trust Lolly to flesh this Fire-Food thing out. The Girls, meanwhile, were still digesting the Fire-Food sneak attack. History had shown they were uncomfortable with spontaneous artistic turns, so this could very well throw the apple cart off the cliff. Kathy raised her hand, and I braced for the worst.

"Yes Kathy," Lolly said, pointing to her.

"Will she be billed as Fire-Food in the program?"

"Yes." She paused. "Any more questions?"

Lolly looked around and waited a good 30 seconds for another question, but nobody moved. Kathy had sabotaged us. In the face of such confusion, she had asked a ludicrous question, leaving us newly dumbfounded at its absurdity.

"Great," Lolly pressed on. "Now, I've written a song about fucking geese that I want to put into the piece."

I immediately laughed. I find rhymes funny. Geese, piece. Call me eight years old, but any time someone rhymes, I laugh. Everyone else was silent. What was this woman talking about?

"When you say 'fucking geese,' do you mean like, 'those God-damned fucking geese' or 'copulating birds'?" I asked. The way she inflected "fucking," it could have gone either way.

"No, it's not about geese having sex. It's a song about men having sex with geese."

Oh. Of course! That cleared everything up. It was a poem about bestiality. That's exactly what this play about 20th-century literati needed.

In all fairness, if it was about *burning* geese, I might have followed the logic. That might actually have brought some meaning to this Fire-Food character. But as it was presented, I felt it to be a bit harsh. It wasn't fair. The stealth of the Fire-Food introduction followed by the crudeness of goose-fucking was too much to process. Besides, both concepts seemed completely detached from each other and, more importantly, from our story. These new ideas added nothing but distractions.

Lolly handed out the new text, which proved to be very funny, and, as it turned out, a great illustration of the hedonistic decadence of the early 1920s. Did it fit into our show? Doubtful. Is it true the titans of industry sat around copulating with geese and breaking their necks at the point of climax? Anything is possible, but we were fairly certain none of our characters had engaged in this behavior.

I couldn't figure it out. This was how Lolly chose to start the rehearsal process? By sitting us down and introducing a character called Fire-Food and a song about fucking geese? Didn't we already have enough to think about? Weren't we already confused? We all felt as though Lolly was fucking up the show. As we left the rehearsal that evening, I thought about giving Lolly a tub of Vaseline with a note that read, "This isn't prison, please use generously," but opted, instead, to bite on my pencil.

Two weeks later, when I arrived at the rehearsal room, I noticed a strange man sitting next to Lolly. He was wearing glasses with thick black rims. By the exchange of snickers and whispers between them, I could tell trouble was brewing.

Rehearsals had been going OK. Lolly was demanding, but she kept things moving. She had given the scenes we'd written a very clear style, one with specific movement and highly intentional dialogue delivery. It was almost presentational, but we didn't address the audience the way a mime or a clown would. It was more like a continuous wink, subtly letting the audience know we knew they were there and "in" on something. She had choreographed the opening, where we emerge one-by-one from a coffin-shaped piano. The effect would leave the audience wondering just how many people can squeeze into one coffin.

"Welcome, everyone," Lolly said, clapping her hands. "Before we start today, I want to introduce everyone to my friend Harrison. He's going to be watching rehearsal today, and if there is something someone can't do, like a handstand, for instance, he is here to replace you. Man or woman, it doesn't matter. We'll put him in a dress. He doesn't care. He just wants to work."

We all knew this was targeted squarely at Deborah, our Zelda, a physically and emotionally demanding part that, I believe, every lady in the room— including Lolly—was dying to play. During a lively dance to the goose-fucking song, Zelda was supposed to spring upside-down and walk around on her hands, her dress and crinoline falling over her torso to create the body of the bird, and her feet in yellow slippers to represent the bill.

"This is a very clever bit of imagery," I had whispered to Lolly when she first presented the idea.

"I fucking hate clever," Lolly replied. "I'll make sure it doesn't come off as clever. Clever is for comedians. I'm a serious artist, and this is serious art."

I chuckled. Nothing is funnier than a serious artist trying to be serious when she's making her serious art.

Sadly, in our circumstance, it didn't much matter if it was serious or clever. Deborah could not perform a handstand. She'd turn upside-down, her legs would flail about for a few seconds, and then she'd collapse to the floor. We watched her try for 10 solid minutes. After each fall, she'd brush herself off, quickly think through what went wrong, and try again.

Twenty-five attempts later, she announced, exhaustedly, that she would practice more at home but was doubtful she'd master it by opening. I thought she was very gallant in her efforts, but we had "Lubeless Lolly" as a director. If Deborah could not stand on her hands, this Harrison guy would walk on *his* hands right into the coveted role. He even demonstrated his handstand abilities for a nauseating two minutes.

Lolly may have thought it was funny, but I was angry at her for pulling this stunt. I certainly wasn't going to fault the rest of the cast for not wanting to mine their way to some mysterious point I'm sure Lolly could have illuminated in a million better ways.

After rehearsal, I walked to the train with Lolly and Harrison.

"Listen, Lolly, you have to pull back," I warned her. "Folks are getting really upset. Frankly, I'm surprised nobody quit tonight."

"I don't care. They're not trying, Randy. They're not even trying."

"They *are* trying. Just because they can't do everything you want them to doesn't mean they're not trying."

"Oh, they're just making excuses. They can do it. They're not trying hard enough. They should get past all their internal blocks and just do what I ask." Lolly stopped. "I'm the director!"

"Yeah. Sure. You are the director. Which means you have to direct us, not berate us. You've got to let go of some of that Landmark Forum crap and start really leading."

Lolly paused at my desecration of the Forum, a cult-like self-empowerment organization spawned by Werner Erhard's est, but I continued.

"And don't forget that some of these people are also the writers and producers of this play. We're creating this thing together, and you have to work with them. If someone can't do something, change it! No more, 'This is my friend Harrison' bullshit. It's childish, and it's dirty. No offence, Harrison."

"I'm dirty," said Harrison, smiling. "So, no offence taken."

"But they can't do a handstand!" Lolly shouted. "Why should I have to compromise my vision because they can't do something? You see how resistant they are to my ideas. You know they're going to question everything I say."

"They're not physical performers, Lolly. They're just not. Let's work with what we've got, OK?"

"I hate them," Lolly said in resignation.

"I'm pretty sure they hate you too," I replied.

"Well, at least everyone knows where they stand. That's one thing we've got going for us."

The situation felt pathetic. We both recognized it and agreed we'd continue the work sans any more "This is my friend Harrison" crap.

With production in full swing, my schedule was non-stop from 8 a.m. to midnight. We had a set, costumes, lighting, and sound designers all fast at work. Thanks to the spectacular photos and some momentum from the FringeNYC festival, *The Expatriates* was getting a lot of press. Bobby, as publicity manager, had done an amazing job of printing postcards—which we now produced by the thousands—posters, and advertisements which were all placed in every theater lobby, coffee shop, and bar in town.

More than 20 people were working on the production, twice as many as on our previous shows. Our venue had grown, too. FringeNYC had placed us in the Kraine Theater, the 99-seat proscenium stage at 85 East Fourth Street. The first-floor theater, more seats, and fewer stairs—if you weren't in our inner circle, you'd say The Beggars Group was going strong.

Two weeks before opening and four weeks into rehearsals, the actress playing Fire-Food called me from a payphone near some basketball courts in Chelsea.

"Randy, I really need your help," she pleaded. "I'm at a pay phone by the basketball courts on 22nd Street. What are you doing right now?"

She was clearly upset, but why was she at a basketball court?

"What's going on?"

"I just really need your help. Can you meet up with me? I don't know what I'm doing."

I wanted to say, "You're playing Fire-Food, how hard can that be? Just burn and eat baby, burn and eat!" But I knew better than to tease a desperate woman. Instead, I agreed to meet her at court number three, wherever that was.

When I arrived, she was sitting on a park bench, slumped over, mumbling incoherently. If I didn't recognize her, I'd have sworn she was a crazy homeless woman.

"Well, it looks like you've got this part nailed," I said, sitting next to her.

"Randy, thank God you're here. Help me! I'm so confused. I don't know where I fit into this play! I keep asking Lolly, and she keeps talking about nourishment and how I fuel life."

"And fire…" I interrupt. "The fire is death. How you take life away."

"Yes! And while that makes perfect sense when we talk about it, I don't know how that's supposed to justify my presence on stage."

She stood up, looked around, paranoid, and whispered, as if the pigeons contained recording devices, "I mean, what am I doing in this play?"

Her eyes were crazy. She had a hopeless look I read as the first move toward walking away from the project. A jolt of dread shot through me.

By this time, I no longer had faith that Lolly could bring reason to this Fire-Food business. Fire-Food was dragging the play into a performance-art realm not unlike watching naked lesbians smear peanut butter on one breast, jelly on the other, and…

But I couldn't tell this to Fire-Food. A civil war was breaking out inside The Beggars Group, with Fire-Food as the wild card that kept everyone off balance. The perfect distraction, Fire-Food was like an alien spaceship landing in the field at the battle of Gettysburg. The North and the South still wanted to kill each other, but what the hell was that round metal object floating off the ground over there?

If Fire-Food left, the play might take a turn for the better, but then Lolly and The Girls would be forced to reconcile their differences, a process I was certain would end badly. I had to preserve this delicate balance for the sake of the play. So, I rolled up my sleeves and dug in.

We worked for two hours: reciting poems, running around the court, screaming at the top of our lungs, doing cartwheels. We did sense-memory exercises, improv games, and after we had tried everything we could think of, we sat on the bench to catch our breath.

"Randy, I feel so much better. Right now, anyway."

"Yeah, that was fun."

"I still don't know where I fit in the play."

"You don't," I said, and she looked at me hard.

"No, I don't."

"That wasn't a question. I said you don't. You don't fit into this play, and you have to stop trying to figure it out. You'll just drive yourself crazy."

She looked at me, wanting more. I didn't have more, so I just rearranged the words and repeated myself.

"Fit. This play. You don't. Crazy yourself will drive." My fun was serving no one but myself. "You shouldn't be in the play. You have no place in it. But you are in it, so just do what you're gonna do, and stop worrying about it."

"Wow, Randy, that was honest," said Fire-Food, with great relief.

I could see her carrying the weight of the whole play on her shoulders. She believed somehow, if she didn't understand why Fire-Food was there, the whole play would be ruined. But now she was free to just be Fire-Food, whatever that meant to her, and move on, play be damned. I left her there, dancing around the court exploring the levity of lapping flames. The best ones she'd done all day.

Per Lolly's request, our first technical rehearsal was to be more of a dress rehearsal. We hadn't actually worked in the space, and the set pieces were all brand new to us, but with only two rehearsals in the theater before we opened, we needed to make the most of our time. In full costume and make-up, I crouched inside the coffin-shaped piano, clutching a fistful of papers, waiting for my cue. Mere moments before I was to pop up through the lid throwing papers, Lolly stopped the action to make some adjustments.

We were only 10 minutes into the play, and she'd stopped us at this place at least 15 times already. It's not unusual to stop often in a technical rehearsal, but very few of her adjustments had actually been technical. Lolly stopped our rehearsal to give direction to the actors, all of whom had been expertly biting their tongues. Meanwhile, I'd been crouching inside this coffin/piano for a good 40 minutes. Each time we stopped, I'd adjust my position a little to prevent my legs from falling asleep. Patience is the actor's backbone. I just had to breathe and relax.

"Lolly!" a shout came from the booth. "This is OUR rehearsal! You can work on acting stuff outside the theater!" The stage manager finally asserted herself. "Please, let us get through this so we know what we're doing."

Everyone on stage smiled as Lolly marched back into the darkened audience. Watching her slink into her seat, I realized Lolly was just as unhappy directing as everyone else was about her directing. She didn't want to be in the audience. She wanted to be on stage. She wanted to perform. The reasons for her behavior suddenly came into focus.

The action resumed, and once again, I adjusted my squat, poised to jump. Finally, I heard my cue, threw open the coffin lid, stood up, and began tossing papers into the air. "Manifesto..." was the last thing I heard myself say.

Here's a short history of all the times I've passed out.

Once, when I was an altar boy, I locked my knees during the endless Christmas mass communion. Some lovely old lady, who had noticed my sways, caught me before I hit my head.

Second, I passed out in a bar bathroom. The toilet seat had cut off circulation to my legs and when I stood, everything went black. Nobody caught me that time. Instead, I awoke to angry knocks on the door demanding for me to hurry.

Third, I fainted into a snowdrift. I looked up at a billboard in the middle of a snowy New York night and, for no reason, I just slumped over. Maybe it was aliens? Maybe I was mugged? A snow bank broke my fall that time.

And fourth, I passed out after smoking some super-sticky skunkweed, which, I'm convinced, could have tranquilized a whale.

And now, Fainting Number Five.

The actual passing out is rather uneventful. Usually everything gets fuzzy, like the snow on an un-tuned television, and then everything stops. The real excitement comes when you wake up. Your position has shifted. Time has skipped. And it takes a few moments to regain self-awareness.

I opened my eyes to see a group of white ghoul-like faces with crazy eye makeup lit very brightly from behind. They were all staring down at me as if I were some unusual road kill. I glanced toward my feet and saw my torso encased in a coffin. Unsure of what was up and down, I couldn't tell if I was rising out of, or falling into, this container. I heard someone running away, shouting for an ambulance, and everything came back into focus.

"Don't call an ambulance," I said in my fullest voice. "I'm going to be fine. Just give me a second to catch my breath."

I reassured everyone I had simply been squatting too long and, when I jumped up, my blood pressure had probably dropped too fast. It was nothing to worry about, and I demanded we all get back to work.

The Girls took this fainting spell as a sign. A sign Lolly had hijacked the show. Her potential to cause physical harm was illustrated by my dramatic tumble out of the coffin.

They were right. Lolly had hijacked the show. I couldn't argue with that, but we had built this airplane together, and The Girls needed to have a little more faith in its construction. The plane may not land where we wanted it to, but it wasn't going to crash. The show was going to go on. Babies were not going to die. We were just making theater.

We managed to finish the rehearsal, get our notes from Lolly, and leave the theater by 6 p.m. Bobby and I had been home for 15 minutes when the call came from The Girls. They were convening an important meeting, not about feelings, in their office building at 9 p.m.

And that's how The Girls lured Lolly, Bobby, and I to this downtown office conference room, where we had no real business being in the first place.

The Girls congregated in the bathroom for almost a half-hour before Kathy emerged and asked to speak with me privately. We made ourselves comfortable in Jonathan Klein's office. You could tell Jonathan Klein was a big shot by the photos of his perfect family, perfect boats, and perfect views of the harbor. New Jersey's skyline is such a disappointment.

Kathy apologized for coaxing me downtown under false pretences and realized that, after the fainting episode, I should have been resting. But she, too, was terribly concerned about her own physical well-being. I recognized this as either total horseshit or some weird appropriation of another person's feelings, as her role as Sara Murphy was the least physical part in the show. But I let it pass and apologized for raising my voice at her.

We agreed we had all worked too hard to let the project fall apart now, and while our differences of opinion were most likely permanent, we did have Fire-Food to consider. Not to mention the rest of the cast, who'd all put in so much time and energy. With the shake of our hands, we decided to forge on with the understanding we would discuss everything once the show closed. Then, and only then, would we all sit down and have a postmortem, where feelings of all kinds could run wild.

When we emerged, Andrea was handing out car-service vouchers as a peace offering. Free rides home in the backseats of black sedans waiting downstairs, compliments of the Investment Bank. Of this you can be sure: Running a ragtag theater company requires resilience and resourcefulness. And working at a bank generates a deep well of both.

POSTMORTEMS KILL

Show time! The largest endeavor of The Beggar Group's short history is about to begin. After more than a year, over 1,000 man-hours, countless involuntary corporate donations, and an endless supply of will, we'd finally arrived. FringeNYC was in full swing.

With the drama of the rehearsal process now behind us, we Beggars put on our best faces. We spent the first two days checking out other FringeNYC shows, handing out postcards, and drumming up as much business as we could. And those efforts paid off.

Our first audience was quite large and, like most festival audiences, hard-core and very vocal. Most had probably seen two other shows earlier that day and would see another after dinner. These were theatrical connoisseurs, an ideal audience to test our new show.

The lights dim, and the show begins with our stylistic exhuming of our characters through the coffin-shaped piano. It's alternately weird and funny, and the audience chuckles. Once the ghoulish overture finishes, the play begins in earnest. The audience seems engaged during the first 10 minutes, which is mostly well-written exposition, fast and crisp, crucial for an hour-long play. The audience laughs at the appropriate moments, and attentively listens to our characters' frustrations surrounding Zelda's book. Surprisingly, they love the goose-fucking song. I don't know if it was the break in the rhythm of the play, or its naughty nature, but they laugh and even clap when it ends.

And then, 15 minutes into the show, Fire-Food makes her entrance. Bare-breasted and intense, she stomps onto the stage with all the presence of Medea. Taking her place center stage, she lets out a cry that sets off car alarms on East Fourth Street. Everything on stage literally screeches to a halt as she gives birth to Zelda's book. With great moans and screams, she pulls from underneath her flowing skirt a large prop book filled with blue pages. Her performance is so realistic, the absence of blood is shocking.

Temporarily deafened by Fire-Food's labor sounds, the biblio-birth puts our audience on the defensive. "And here comes the Living Theater crap," I hear a woman in the audience mutter.

Fire-Food literally stops the show. She just stops the whole fucking show. There may as well have been a 6.5 earthquake right under the building. The cord that connected the play with the audience has been cut, and this was just the beginning of the fun. Things only got stranger. Although it's all very visually interesting, little of it makes much sense, and most of it has nothing to do with the play we'd so neatly set up.

We all take turns pulling and tearing at Zelda's masterpiece. As the book gets destroyed, its blue pages spill out, transforming into a kind of Chinese New Year dragon that is to represent, of all things, a blue lobster. Then, we tell an allegorical tale about a man named Gabius Apitious who consumes himself...or the lobster consumes him. To this day, I'm unsure of the allegory's meaning.

Fire-Food continues to wander the stage reciting poems, part *Girls Gone Wild* and part *King Lear* lost in the storm. But the story—you know, the one about Zelda and F. Scott Fitzgerald, Ernest Hemingway, and Dorothy Parker—gets thrown to the side of the stage to make way for peanut-butter-and-jelly boobs. Mind you, we are all still on stage, saying lines and staying in character. But the show now measures five parts black-and-white '20s film, one part '70s living-theater chic, and a dash of LSD, just to spice it all up.

Thankfully, during the last 10 minutes, we return to the story—that story we started telling before Fire-Food and her lapping flames interrupted us. But by this point in our arc, the fruit is rotten. We return to reality just in time to see our characters bear the brunt of life's cruelties. Sara Murphy's children die. Scott can't control his alcoholism. Dorothy Parker battles her howling horrors, and Ernest Hemingway blows his head off. The death montage does its best to wipe away any memories of the chaotic middle section, and maybe we win back a few audience members who dig the macabre, but we'd already asked quite a lot from them, and most would just shake their heads.

Afterward, at the bar, the cast worked at forgetting the show one pint at a time, but Fire-Food was all anyone talked about. Zelda who? Hemingway what? The only thing you could hear above the clatter of glasses and conversation was, "What the fuck was with that Fire-Food chick?"

Oddly, nobody hates the show. Everyone was entertained, and it might have been due to that fascinating puzzle known as Fire-Food. People couldn't tell if they loved her or hated her, but one thing was certain, she had stolen the show. She was just a concept after all. But she managed to upstage even the best writers of the century.

The festival seemed to end almost as soon as it started. Ten days of nonstop theater-going, theater-making, and theater parties can fly by in the blink of an eye. And we enjoyed it as much as we could, knowing that a sobering reality awaited us on the other side. Two days after we moved the coffin-shaped piano facade (now in the role of a coffee table) into my living room, we assembled at Andrea's downtown apartment for *The Expatriates* post-mortem.

In my mind, Lolly and I would walk into Andrea's apartment, sit down, and listen to The Girls rip us apart, limb from limb, with a sundry of verbal torture devices. Lolly and I, armed with leather straps in our mouths, would wince and whine but take our licks without protestation. We'd ask a few questions, the answers of which we already knew, and leave. It was sick, but we'd prepared for this, expected it, and kind of needed it to bring the experience to a conclusion.

Instead, The Girls greeted us with smiles, offered some wine, and treated us to a casual yet spirited conversation about wheels.

During the course of that first year, we'd had many conversations about wheels, more specifically, how we didn't wish to re-invent them. Whenever we struggled with something, we would call for outreach and research. Someone, somewhere, had done that particular task, and we needed to learn from this person and do it that way too. No need to re-invent.

I'm confident this is a common theme with any new organization. When starting something new, you deal with a great number of strikingly similar variables to the ones faced by your peers and predecessors as well as variables unique to your organization. Sometimes, it pays to take someone else's wheel. But sometimes, another's wheel won't fit, and so you invent a new wheel.

"That's not the point!" Andrea said in a calm but direct voice. "A wheel is a wheel. When I say we shouldn't re-invent the wheel, I mean we shouldn't spend our time trying to work out something that has already been worked out. We should be building from what other people have already done. Why don't you get that?"

Lolly was writing fiercely in her notebook. We'd told each other that taking notes during this meeting would be a good idea. Although we wanted to remember the conversation for future reference, we also wanted to demonstrate we were taking this conversation seriously. But, most importantly, this pen and pad created a physical barrier between us and them. It was our leather strap. We could be grounded firmly behind our paper, frantically writing their answers to the questions we would alternately ask. When Andrea talked, I wrote, "Andrea is right. So why does that make me so angry? I like inventing wheels. I like inventing wheels. I like inventing wheels."

"So, what did you enjoy the most about this project?" Lolly asked. She and I had strategically designed this question to bring levity into the room. "I really enjoyed the writing process," Deborah said. Kathy and Andrea quickly agreed. "It was the first time I've attempted to write dialogue, and I'm proud of what we did."

"That was a great process," I added. This launched the conversation into how much people learned about writing styles, writing in groups, and their own individual desires to continue writing. It was safe territory because it was the only part of the process in which Lolly did not play a major role. She remained quiet until the conversation died down.

"So, what can I, as the director, do to improve?" Lolly asked.

"Don't direct," Deborah said quickly. This was followed by an overwhelming silence, a silence that shouted in agreement. I had told her not to ask the question. While being tortured, it's foolish to expose your most sensitive bits. But I was wrong. It was as if they were anticipating this question and had nominated Deborah to deliver the two-word directive from the group.

"Is there anything else I should know?" Lolly asked, disappointed she hadn't received the bludgeoning she was expecting.

"Nope," Deborah said. "You just shouldn't do it."

"Randy, do you have anything to add to that?" Lolly asked, hoping someone would relieve her of this aching need for abuse.

"I think you had a hard time finding your voice with this group and you failed to overcome that."

I'll admit, I'm lousy at torture.

"How do you mean exactly?"

"Well, look around you. Nobody liked working with you, everyone had a miserable experience, and the play wasn't genius. In my opinion, the only time it's OK for a director to be an asshole is when her work is genius." I was finding my stride.

"Well, next time, it will be genius."

"Yeah, right! In that case, I amend my statement. It is never acceptable for a director to be an asshole. Nobody should be an asshole, ever."

I realized everyone was staring at me hard. Was it irony, or just attention? I couldn't tell, so I changed the subject.

"Now, before we continue, we need to address the future. As you all know, we've booked Under St. Marks for three weeks in October to produce the second incarnation of *The Expatriates*. We have a lot of work to do in the next month, and we need to know now who will be joining us for this production. Let's go around the room and see who is committed to the next production. Lolly, we'll start with you."

"I'm in," said Lolly.

After that came a round of seven "no's" and then one "yes"—from me.

"Well...I would like to invite you all to *The Expatriates* puppet show Randy and I will be presenting in October," said Lolly. The group laughed loudly.

The lack of future participants didn't surprise me, but where was the angst? Where were the feelings? Where was all the crying and venting we'd experienced just weeks before?

"There is something else we need to discuss," Kathy started in a serious tone. Ah, here we go, they made us wait, but we were going to get ours. "I will no longer be a part of this company. I feel disrespected, unappreciated, and abused. And I no longer want to participate."

"OK," I said preparing for the next defection, which came quickly from Andrea, followed by Deborah, then Bobby. They all gave their reasons for not wanting to continue with the company. With the exception of Bobby, who simply wasn't interested in making theater anymore, all expressed disappointment with Lolly and with my handling of the company.

We sat there, Lolly and I, and listened to all the ways we erred. Everyone was very matter-of-fact about everything. There were no tears, no screaming, and no emotions. Just a series of well-prepared statements. And as much as I knew they hated Lolly and had lost respect for me, their comments focused on improving the company—a company that would not include them. It was very mature, and it burned my skin like a hot light bulb. Taking the high road turned out to be far more insidious and hurtful than any tongue-lashing they could have administered.

When they finished, we all stood in unison. It was odd, but we started as an ensemble, and it was only appropriate that we end as one. Everyone began saying their goodbyes with hugs and pleasantries. I was a little pissed off by the civil nature of the evening and was smarting from feeling like an asshole. I stopped in the entryway.

"Kathy, I feel like we've missed something here. I thought we were going to express ourselves more. You know, have that talk about our feelings."

She looked at me very calmly.

"Randy, do you want to talk about your feelings?"

"No, not really."

"Then, why would we want to talk to you about *our* feelings?"

"I don't know, because you had so many feelings before. Because you said you wanted to talk about them then."

I just didn't get it. Where was the climax? If there was no climax, there would be no catharsis. The Beggars Group's splitting was a big fucking deal. I needed catharsis!

"Randy, you have terrible emotional timing. Feelings don't turn on and off like a faucet."

I chuckled a little thinking about Bobby's faucet but quickly regained composure.

"You have to talk about them when you're having them. I needed to talk to you about my feelings then, when I was feeling them. Not now that I've already worked through them. Just like it took a full week after your boyfriend dumped you before you had a meltdown. He wanted you to talk about your feelings then, when you broke up, not a week after you left him. You're too late, Randy. It's over. We're done. You missed your chance to work it out, just like you did with C.J. Now, have a good night."

She closed the door. I felt like I'd just been punched in the face. I had the urge to spit. I just knew my mouth was filling with blood. Was I missing a few teeth? I was unprepared for the hit. With my notebook in my bag, my defenses were down. I stood there for a moment until Lolly grabbed my hand and pulled me into the hot summer night. Kathy was right. I had bad emotional timing.

"Well, *that* was crazy," I said to Lolly, lighting a cigarette as we exited the building.

"Come on, we knew that was going to happen. Give me a cigarette." Lolly didn't even smoke. "That was a really dick thing for Kathy to say. I'm sorry."

"Well, yeah. I guess. But I think she was right."

"Still, it was a really mean thing to do, bring up your ex and all. But hey, if it's true, you're not going to cry about it until next week, right?"

Thank God Lolly was there to lighten the mood. It had been an intense 15 months. We spent a lot of time together, and the cinematic montage of "the good times" was playing in my head.

"So, I totally feel like an asshole, but I don't feel sad. Why do you suppose that is?" I asked, genuinely confused by my emotional state. Lolly was much more practical about it.

"Do you think they're upset? Of course not. They're relieved. They're glad to be rid of us."

"But do you think they're glad to be rid of the company?"

In this instance, I couldn't separate myself from the company. Sure, they were glad to be rid of us, but we took the company. Everything they worked for was now squarely in our hands. It was like a divorce. We all got married, bought a house, fixed it up, had some kids. Lolly beat them, while I stood idly by, then they left. They filed for divorce and just walked away. We got to keep the house, the kids, and everything. I didn't understand how they could be OK with that. Were they really going to be happy? Was their happiness as intrinsically tied to making theater as mine was? The ease of their abandonment shocked me.

"They don't want to do this, Randy. They say they do, but they don't really want to run a theater company."

Maybe Lolly was right. Maybe they had had their experience and were glad to be done with it. Maybe they just wanted to be actors, not publicists, producers, fundraisers, and everything else that comes with running a theater company. This thought provided some clarity, and opened a door for a new emotion. Maybe we needed to pare down the company a bit. Maybe fewer people would give us a better focus. If Lolly and I could just synch our visions, we might actually be able to spring back from this.

"I'm pretty excited," I said, looking over at Lolly, who was already smiling from ear to ear.

"Me too," she replied. It dawned on me that we had a lot to be excited about. Despite having no cast and no producing team, we *did* have a few things going for us. We had three weeks fully paid for at Under St. Marks Theater in October, all the publicity materials printed, several thousand dollars in the bank, and another four weeks at Under St. Marks half-paid for in April. Basically, we were sitting on an entire season of infrastructure that had been laid out and mostly funded. This was the house that The Girls and Bobby left behind. And Lolly and I had the urge to redecorate.

"So, about the next show," I began. "You can't direct it."

"I know," she said. And we walked all the way home to West 109th Street, carefully plotting the new incarnation of The Beggars Group.

RETURN OF THE JAZZ AGE

"The war to end all wars has ended," I say to the audience, as I emerge from inside the large fireplace on stage. "And Americans everywhere are celebrating! Many U.S. citizens have moved overseas where the dollar is strong and life is easy. These days, fashionable Paris is filled to the brim with American artists and intellectuals who have found a new home in the city of lights. We caught this glittering crowd..."

A loud banging from stage left interrupts me. On the other side of the red-framed glass door, the ghostly faces of Zelda, F. Scott, Ernest, and Dorothy plead to be granted entrance. After several more interruptions, I acquiesce, and the literary luminaries, with Big Eye makeup, burst onto the stage to tell their stories.

The Beggars Group had begun a transformation. We no longer subscribed to the traditional mechanics of making theater. We were moving into a highly collaborative, egoless space of creation. We were no longer operating with titles. There was no director, and nobody would be credited as the writer. It was a play created and presented by The Beggars Group. Sure, if you walked into a rehearsal and asked someone who the director was, they'd probably point to Lolly or me, but we'd deny it. We insisted on clearing the proverbial stage to allow for deeper participation from all the artists in the room.

As the characters dance their way onto the stage, I look up and see Dickey in the booth. Aside from Lolly and me, every face of the new Beggars Group is a fresh one. A week after the company split, I met Dickey at Saints, my local watering hole, where I processed the company's troubles with a small group of friends. When Dickey overheard the conversation, he immediately introduced himself, his technical theater experience, and his desire to hone his fund-raising skills.

It's strange how simply these things happen sometimes. Lolly and I had spent hours fretting over finding the right people to join the company, and here a key player simply walked up and introduced himself as if cued by a divine stage manager.

I give him a nod, and with a clap, the lights on stage change.

Not only was the show different, so was the theater. Located on East Eighth Street (or St. Marks Place), Under St. Marks is one of those theaters you could walk by 100 times and never know it was there. A small marquee at eye level hangs next to a set of stairs that leads to the 50-seat black-box venue in the basement. Rumor has it that before becoming a theater in the 1980s, the space was a den for a coven of witches.

Its many unique details—the narrow stairwell descending into the musty subterranean space, the red-framed glass door, exposed plumbing that snakes across the ceiling, and a stage-right wall made entirely out of crumbling red brick—make it the perfect backdrop for our play set in purgatory.

"No, no, no, no, no, no," says Jenny, as her pitch-perfect Dorothy Parker. "I'm serious, George!"

She is referring to Zelda's obsession with ballet-dancing, a historically more accurate and visually more interesting replacement for her book as the central focus of the play.

"Of course, I saw her," Dorothy continues. "The sight was not a flattering one. She looked tall and awkward, and there was something grotesque about her intensity. One could see her muscles stretch and pull. Her legs looked muscular and ugly. One held one's breath until it was over."

Jenny, another miracle find, required a little more searching. After we had alienated most of our friends, Lolly and I needed to cast the show the old-fashioned way—through auditions. Finding actors in New York City is a daunting challenge, not because there is a lack of talent, but because there is such a glut of it.

One ad in the trade paper immediately inundated us with headshots. My mailman even scolded me, demanding I get a P.O. box to receive such huge volumes of mail. How were we supposed to know 500 people wanted to be in our nonpaying off-off-Broadway play in a basement? Two solid days of sifting through piles finally narrowed us down to a reasonable number of actual auditions. We spent a full day seeing people, and the moment Jenny walked into the room, we knew she was our Dorothy.

Jenny and I finish our scene just in time for Harrison, playing F. Scott, to stumble into the action.

"George, I hope tonight is a really terrible party. I hope someone begins throwing up in the toilet closet. I hope there are infidelities and bad manners and fistfights and sodomy. I hope there is a murder! I'm bored of the suffocating Paris salons filled with the literati pontificating, discussing whose farts are the more artistic!"

After he speaks for a short spell, I clap my hands and the scene shifts.

George Antheil, now the ringleader of the production, keeps our characters in line by stopping scenes before they go too far. Besides the tuxedo and my brilliant command of the stage, what separates me from the others is the two Xs on my cheeks. Yes, the Xs have made a comeback.

The theory behind the Xs is still a little all over the place. You could say once a character realizes he needs to let go of his past and move on, his face is X'd out and he is allowed to disappear into the fireplace. Why would someone want to do that? We didn't know. But we decided not to think about it too much. We decided to be intentional in our vagueness. We wanted to give the audience something to think about. So as not to confuse them too much, we lay it all out with a little song, backed by a brilliant three-piece improv jazz band called the Gold Sparkles.

"I am dead! Do you hear me folks? That's what I said. No one wants to die, but they do. And perhaps you will die someday, too."

The Gold Sparkles were Lolly's idea. She was adamant we have live music at all our shows. Canned music is what you get when you go to the movies. Live music is what you should get when you go to live theater. The only problem with live music, though, is that you need musicians. And unlike actors, it's hard to find musicians who will work for free.

Lolly had seen one of the Gold Sparkle's shows and immediately fell in love with them—more specifically, with Charles, the band's leader. So, she invaded her savings account and secured their services for a whopping 2,000 dollars. I didn't have that kind of money, but I can safely say they were worth every penny of Lolly's. They gave the piece a texture and resonance that provided for our viewers a passport to the roaring '20s.

Finally, Zelda enters the fray. Extra dolled up and ready to play, Lolly springs onto the stage with all the life of an 18-year-old.

"I am a salamander who can walk through the hottest of fires," she says to Scott from atop the fireplace. "You're the one who sings across the meadow. The one with the red hair."

While we still aren't making a whole play about Zelda's descent into madness, we are certainly playing with it more. Starting with her growing manic obsessions, we follow her progression until she is sent off to the hospital. Lolly is so fully committed and so wonderfully talented, watching this fall into madness is frightening.

Harrison would throw her down to the floor in one of their dramatic fights, and the theater would shake. A clap from George's hands would stop everything, and we'd change on a dime to a happier time.

The scene-shifts are quick and clean and highly stylized, thanks to another Beggars Group newcomer.

Fannie is an attractive, extremely charismatic, and highly aggressive woman. With a cartoonishly high-pitched voice, she is at once an excitable and thoughtful "Daddy's little princess" slumming in the city. She also happens to be a great dancer with big ideas, so Lolly and I enlisted her to help with the movement. She rounded out our team of young, bold, and committed theatrical practitioners.

After a few scenes of some lighter moments, like Scott worrying that the size of his penis can't satisfy his wife (a fear he cures by showing his pecker to Hemingway), the play concludes just as the previous version had, by wading through the darker periods of our characters' lives. Howling horrors Dorothy. Shotgun Hemingway. And Zelda, losing touch with reality, slips away from her husband and the world. "I was supposed to be…" says Zelda, striking her best ballet third position and reaching out to her husband.

"You were supposed to be my heroine," he replies, as he Xs his face and disappears into the fireplace.

The show is still a little too abstract for some theatergoers, but we were finding our style, and the audience members who get it, really get something.

But most importantly, we were invigorating artists and generating a tremendous amount of energy around the company. Making theater is contagious. This is probably true of many things, but of theater I am certain. And people around us were getting the bug.

After the show, we'd pack our props while the Gold Sparkles riffed, and then we'd head out into the East Village in search of a warm place to eat, drink, and imitate the brighter events of our subjects' lives. When I look back to that time, my favorite picture is the silhouette of Lolly and Charles lagging behind to kiss under a streetlight.

"The war to end all wars has ended, and people everywhere are celebrating."

Part IV
DO IT!

THE ALIENS HAVE LANDED

I have no idea what is going on. I never see any portal open. No passage from outer space. I certainly don't see any aliens. Maybe I'm not supposed to see aliens and portals. Maybe I have to be stoned out of my mind. Or maybe I just have to believe. But I'm not on drugs, and I just can't get myself to believe that the wild group of people running around the stage in ridiculous costumes and body paint are aliens. And to make matters worse, they keep asking me to join them. They want me to participate. The more they ask, the more I resist. I hole myself up in the technical booth of Under St. Marks Theater protected by a nest of cables. Someone has to run the lights.

I was all for producing a "happening" to promote our next show, *Do It!,* but what is going on down below is not for me. They keep asking, but I am determined NOT to become a Prudenian.

A few months earlier, before the holidays consumed our attention, Lolly and I had spent several days piecing our puzzle of how to fill the four-week slot at Under St. Marks in April. We originally planned a production of George Bernard Shaw's *Major Barbara*. But that was the old Beggars Group. We were the new Beggars Group now, and we needed to find a new project.

"We should do it!" Lolly said, as she bounced a ball off my bedroom ceiling one day.

"Do what exactly?"

"We should do *Do It!*" she smiled, looking at me.

It took me a moment to realize she was talking about *Do It!*, the book written by Yippie founder Jerry Rubin. I'd come across the book years earlier at a used bookstore in Tempe, Arizona. After two minutes of flipping through it, I knew this wild and exciting portrait of the 1960s counterculture movement would make a great play. It's chaptered out perfectly, almost cinematic in its structure. With hundreds of photos and graphics, *Do It!* is exaggerated, impassioned, and wildly entertaining—a book to be experienced rather than simply read. This kind of book floated through college dorm rooms being recited aloud at one o'clock in the morning—which is exactly what happened when I brought it back to my school.

"We should totally do *Do It!*" I repeated as I rifled through my closet to find my copy. Some of the many good things about doing *Do It!*: It's fun, it's funny, and it has plenty of action. But the best part was I'd already tested the book's collaborative applications.

When I was struggling to do something creative in L.A., I invited 10 people to my house to make a show out of the book in 24 hours. We called it Crash Theater, and it worked. We mounted 30 minutes of the book in one day. If it worked in 24 hours, imagine what we could do in several months.

Back at Under St. Marks, the Prudenians prance around the stage in a very loose improvisation of *The Odyssey*. At least that's what they tell me. I can't seem to find the story amongst the chaos. I can't tell which Prudenian is playing which role. Truth be told, they all blend together with their cardboard hats, torn fabric costumes, and sloppy body paint. This show contains all the chaos of a first-grade Halloween parade.

The only people who stand out are the three monks. They stand out because they wear monk cloaks and because they play instruments. They're called the Moon Monks—even though they don't come from Prudenia. They come from Atlanta, so I am told.

Now that we had decided to do *Do It!*, we began a full-blown recruiting campaign. We had pulled off the second production of *The Expatriates* with a little more than a dozen cast and crew, but we knew this next project would require three times that many people.

While Lolly and I shared very similar theatrical visions, our recruiting methods couldn't have been more different. Her idea of generating interest was to produce a portal opening where aliens called Prudenians come to earth to tell an ancient Greek story. My idea of recruiting was...

"Randy!" Lolly said, barreling through the front door of my apartment late one afternoon. "What the fuck is the TBG Development System?"

Bobby was with her but didn't say anything. He just laughed.

"I'm sorry," I said. "What are you talking about?"

"I'm talking about our casting notice." She threw open the paper and read, "Utilizing the TBG Development System, we will create a new and exciting play based on Jerry Rubin's book, *Do It!*"

"Oh, yeah. That's pretty good, don't you think?" I was proud of that ad.

"I like it," Bobby said. "It really sounds like it's something, ya know?"

"Thank you, I thought so too," I replied.

"What is the TBG Development System?" Lolly asked.

Bobby jumped in before I could. "I told you. It's The Beggars Group Development System. And by the way, the font Dickey uses on your business cards makes *tbg* look like *fag*."

"What? Really?"

"Yeah. It's the lower-case italics. The *t* looks like an *f*, and the *b* looks like an *a*. I'm just saying."

"Hmm... or maybe you see 'fag' because you are one," Lolly shouted. "Anyway, we can talk about that later. Right now, we need to deal with this Development System."

I could tell she wasn't angry, but she was getting that look women get just before they make you pull over and ask for directions... and I'm not the kind of guy who asks for directions.

"What's there to talk about?" I asked innocently.

"We don't have a fucking development system!"

Just then, Bobby's pocket began beeping, which caused an uncomfortable pause.

"When did you get a beeper?" I asked.

Bobby ignored me, looked at the number on the pager, and disappeared into his bedroom.

"Why does he have a pager?" I asked Lolly.

"He's hustling now," she replied. "I'm probably not supposed to tell you, but you're gonna find out eventually. So listen, Randy, don't you think this makes it sound like we already have a system?"

"No. Wait. What?"

"It does. It sounds like we have an established system."

"It doesn't say 'the established TBG Development System.' Apparently, it says 'the fag development system.'" I stopped to laugh at my own joke. "No really, it's fine. It's just a gimmick to get people excited. Did you say Bobby is hustling?"

"Yeah. But I don't understand why you felt the need to put that into the notice?"

"Umm." I stopped for a moment. I wanted to learn more about Bobby's new career but didn't feel good about gossiping when he was in the next room. "Look, I wanted to peak people's interest. Without the TBG Development System, the ad felt too loosey-goosey.

Like we weren't serious. I didn't want to attract touchy-feely people. I wanted to attract serious-focused people, and serious-focused people are attracted to systems."

The irony—that this is actually a play about loosey-goosey people—provided even more reason to hire serious-focused people.

"I don't know, Randy." Lolly wasn't convinced, but within hours, our email inbox filled up.

"To Whom It May Concern, I am very interested in learning more about the TBG Development System..." they'd write.

"Does he have a pimp?" I asked.

I couldn't help myself. I'd never known a prostitute before and was curious to learn the mechanics of the profession. Actually, I'd never known a coke addict before Bobby's brief addiction. Bobby was single-handedly introducing me to a whole world of different people. Sadly, that trend would quickly come to an end. A few weeks into his hustling gig, he left the city to become a flight attendant, which was too bad for me. I'd already met plenty of flight attendants.

Our ad garnered enough interest for us to invite 50 people to audition. From that, we found our cast of eight.

When we determined that Noj, one of the 50, was not going to make the final cut, Fannie asked that she be the one to call and tell him—so she could then ask him for a date, arguably the worst pick-up strategy ever. But Fannie's persuasiveness and her ability to seduce were not to be underestimated. Sure enough, she called him, worked her magic, and, within days, they had embarked on an epic romance. This began The Beggars Group's relationship with Prudenia.

My love life had also taken an interesting turn. Since my breakup with C.J., I'd been dating quite a few people. Although the relationships never lasted very long, their intensity ranged from soap-opera hot to Hollywood cool. I was thoroughly combing the New York dating pool, which, for a gay man, is more like an ocean. And then, on December 23, as the holidays approached, I met Scott. Dickey and I were throwing back a few pints in a sparsely occupied Saints when Scott walked in alone. Bars can be lonely places around the holidays, so when I caught sight of his sky-blue eyes, I called him over hoping we'd all feel a little warmer for the company.

What started out very casually quickly morphed into something unrecognizable, exciting, and vastly different from my previous parade of suitors. Then, after three weeks of dating, he sprang it on me.

"So, I'm going to Italy for work in May. Do you want to come over and meet me? Do some sight-seeing."

The offer was exciting and tempting, but May was five months away. Agreeing to go to Italy in five months with someone I'd only been dating for three weeks had high disaster potential. Even my longest relationship struggled to last five months. But his eyes so blue and his dimples so cute and his fun and his smarts and his sanity and his charm and his everything else made me say "yes." I was going to Italy with Scott in May—if we lasted that long.

The Beggars Group's official introduction to Prudenia came through a man named Blue, who is actually Noj, but one is not supposed to think realistically when dealing with this alien planet. Blue is the Prudenian ambassador to Earth. Apparently, he's been coming to our planet on and off for the past couple of years. He even has a pied-à-terre in the city.

Shortly after the *Do It!* auditions, we received a videotape in the mail. It featured a man painted blue from head to toe, wearing nothing but a dance belt, and doing headstands on a busy subway platform—a spectacle not totally uncommon in New York.

"He's got a nice ass...and he can really do a headstand," I said, watching with guarded curiosity.

"I know, right?" Lolly acknowledged.

"That's Noj?"

"Uh-huh."

"Why didn't we cast him?"

"He wasn't right for this play."

"And this is the guy Fannie's dating?"

"Yeah."

"Is this all he does? He paints himself blue and goes around the city doing headstands?"

"No, it gets weirder."

Lolly hit fast-forward. He's in Union Square, on the Brooklyn Bridge, in Central Park. Blue is everywhere. Then, she hit play again to show a crowd of girls in a studio. The video quality had improved, and I could tell it was no longer homemade.

"What's this?" I asked.

"It's *Total Request Live*," Lolly responded.

"The MTV show?"

"Uh-huh."

She suppressed her laughter so I could hear. The host made his rounds through the group, asking each girl a question or two. And then, he got to Blue. Lolly's laughter crescendoed.

"So, whom do we have here?" the host asked the blue-painted man, now wearing a tunic, which I gather the studio people suggested.

"My name is Blue, and I come from Prudenia. I bring a message of peace and love to the people of Earth."

"Of course, he does," I mumbled.

During the brief back and forth between the host and Blue, I lost interest. It was too weird for me, but Lolly—who is, after all, the mother of Fire-Food—craved this kind of artistic expression. She quickly recruited him to run lights for the show, and he quickly recruited *her* to produce this freeform extravaganza called *A Portal Opening*.

Everyone in the company had gotten into the act—which was easy for them. I was the only one with a full-time day job. Dickey, Harrison, Fannie, and Lolly had all been up for days making costumes, piecing together a script, and preparing for the arrival of our friends from another galaxy. Then, the Moon Monks arrived in a Chevy from Atlanta, and their love-fest exploded. I, on the other hand, diligently went to work and line-produced all this craziness. No wonder I was so bitterly holed up in the technical booth as the band of crazies fling themselves around the stage. This is exactly the kind of loosey-gooseyness I had hoped to avoid.

Despite all the chaos, or maybe because of it, The Beggars Group was moving at a thousand miles an hour. Our combined efforts to build a community proved very successful. We produced play-readings, panel discussions, and portal openings. We capitalized on the momentum of each event to build the next. We were moving fast, for sure. And the faster you're going, the more precise your steering needs to be. And wouldn't you know, we all took turns holding the wheel as if we were on a carnival ride.

"Randy!" Blue shouts to me up in the booth. "I love you!"

Instead of replying, I wash the stage in red light and the performers change their movements. They are all so present and susceptible to external stimulation, they appear more like single-cell organisms than highly evolved extraterrestrials. Finally, around midnight, the performance ends, and the portal closes. But the Prudenians would be back, and much to my surprise, I'd become one.

EL BOHIO

By the beginning of March, production for *Do It!* fell into full swing. We rehearsed on Eighth Street and Avenue B in an old four-story schoolhouse called Charas/El Bohio. The space, managed by a community center that had been squatting in the building for some time, cost only five bucks an hour—and we got what we paid for. The rooms, untouched since the children moved out two decades earlier, included cracked and missing tiles, filthy walls, and broken lights. The one working bathroom was one of the dirtiest I'd ever seen in my entire life. Most of us wouldn't go anywhere near it.

"This show is going to kill us!" we'd say every morning as we wiped the filth off our clothes after warm-ups—Pilates, yoga, push-ups, and sit-ups, the menu of morning exercises performed on the school's dirty broken tiles. Then, we'd run our stunts. Under St. Marks is a tiny theater with a low ceiling. But just because you don't have much room doesn't mean you can't create a spectacle. Our spectacle consisted of slow-motion sequences, sideways lifts, inversions, and unison movements. The magic of these stunts lay in the timing and precision, so it was important to spend time perfecting them at every rehearsal. For the rest of the rehearsal, we created the show scene-by-scene based on the book and our research.

Unlike *The Expatriates*, where our research required spending hours in the library, the Yippies called for a different kind of investigation. Yes, people wrote about the Yippies, but not at length and not with the hindsight that a separation of several generations affords. The Yippies and their contemporaries remained very much alive. In fact, they were our college professors and our bosses. This kind of research required a more hands-on approach.

This was why Lolly arrived at Dickey's apartment one Saturday evening clutching a scrap of paper in her sweaty hands. The phone number scribbled on it came from a friend we affectionately called Eric Stoner. Dickey and I watched as she slowly pressed the numbers on the phone.

"Make sure you don't call him the Weed Monkey," Dickey said. "That might piss him off."

"Well, what am I supposed to say?" Lolly asked, hanging up the phone. "I'm not calling, you call." And she thrust the phone into my lap.

"No way. I'm not doing it. It was your idea. You do it." And I threw the phone back to her.

Suddenly, we were back in middle school, passing the phone back and forth as if we were calling a boy one of us secretly liked. But this wasn't a secret boy crush; this was a drug dealer called The Weed Monkey.

Unlike the literary giants of the '20s, where alcohol was the drug of choice, the Yippies preferred marijuana. They smoked a lot of dope. And while we had no interest in smoking a lot of dope, we did feel it necessary to have some marijuana "around" while we worked on the project. Getting stoned on occasion might lend some authenticity to the project. Of course, I'd smoked pot before (see chapters 3 and 5) but actively seeking out and purchasing an illegal substance was totally different. It was participating in the illegal drug trade. It meant danger. And it was thrilling.

Finally, we decided Lolly had more balls than Dickey or I, and she completed the dialing.

"It's ringing," she said, looking at us nervously. "What if he doesn't answer? Do I leave...um, hello." She paused, giving us the "I'm AWAKE" Big Eyes. "I'm a friend of Eric's. He gave me your number. My name is Lolly."

She was doing great, although I would have used a fake name. Dickey and I watched intently.

"Yes. I was wondering if you were going to be around tonight?" The question came out awkward and unsure. She definitely sounded like a first-timer, which could work in our favor, as he'd be sure she wasn't a cop. "Yes. I'm at 109th and Amsterdam...OK. Sure. All right. Great. We'll see you soon." And she hung up. We were all silent for a moment.

"Well?" Dickey said, unable to maintain the requisite tension-building silence.

"He's going to be at the corner in 15 minutes. He's in a black Honda Accord with tinted windows. He'll call when he's there, then we're supposed to go out and get in his car."

"Are you fucking crazy?" I asked. "There's no way we're getting into some drug-dealer's car. He could rob us or kill us."

"Or rape us," Dickey added delightfully, making fun of my prudishness. "Don't worry, Randy. I'll go with Lolly. You can stay here."

I didn't argue. I told myself that someone needed to be home in case they were arrested. Always have someone on the outside. That's a cardinal rule for criminals, and we were now officially criminals.

Our conversation quickly turned to how much we were going to secure and what we thought it might cost. In her haste, Lolly forgot to discuss the business details on the phone (if you could even do that), and we had no point of reference. Getting killed or raped were certainly on the menu of possible outcomes, but getting ripped off was far more likely.

We decided they'd accept 60 bucks. Dickey left his wallet, and Lolly removed her jewelry. They wouldn't even bring keys, lest the drug dealer/thief/thug took them and helped himself to the contents of the apartment—which included me. If he was going to rob them, he'd get the 60 bucks and that was it... well, the 60 bucks and their innocence, if he so chose.

The phone rang, and we jumped out of our skins. Lolly lifted the receiver.

"Hello?" she listened for a moment. "OK. We'll see you in a second." And she hung up the phone. "He's coming up the block."

We all stood up. I gave them each a ceremonial hug and told them I'd call the police if they weren't back in five minutes. The door closed behind them, and I waited. And waited. And waited.

Twenty minutes later, somebody buzzed. I pressed the "listen" button to see if I could determine who was there. I heard Lolly and Dickey talking. Then, I pressed the "talk" button.

"Are you guys OK?"

"Yeah. We're fine," Dickey said. "Let us in."

"Are you alone?" I asked. I was worried the drug dealer/thief/thug had taken them hostage and was using them to gain entrance into the apartment.

"Yes, we're alone. Let us in already."

Still unconvinced, I opened the apartment door. Dickey lived on the first floor, and you could see down the hallway out through the double-glass doors. There, on the stoop, stood Lolly and Dickey.

"Open the fucking door!" they screamed when they saw me peeking down the hall. I pressed the door button, and they burst in.

"What took you guys so long?" I asked. "It's been, like, a half-hour. I was starting to really freak out."

Lolly and Dickey were laughing, but I didn't bother to ask what about.

"We stopped at Saints for a drink," Dickey said. "I thought you said you were going to call the cops if we weren't back in five minutes?"

"Yeah, well...I gave it a little more time."

I mean, really. What would I tell the cops? My two friends were trying to buy drugs and got abducted? I could hear the laughter on the other side of the phone.

"Did you get the stuff?" I asked. Lolly revealed a puffy bag, filled with a quarter-ounce of sticky green buds.

"You guys are rock stars," I said. "I don't want to smoke, but I'll roll a joint if anyone else does."

Lolly and Dickey shook their heads. The excitement was in the securing of the substance, not the substance itself, so we skipped getting stoned and got down to work on the play instead.

The first point of business was to get the scoop straight from the horse's mouth. Since we began the project, I had been in contact with Stew Albert, an original Yippie and a character in Jerry's book. He and his wife were going to be in town, so we arranged to meet up at Ratner's, a Lower East Side deli the Yippies frequented back in the day.

When I arrived, I could see Ratner's days were numbered. The place still possessed a kind of nostalgic charm but was in complete disrepair. I commented on this as I sat down in the booth across from Stew and his wife Judy.

"I know," Stew said. "I hardly recognize it. They've changed so much around. But it's been here since 1905. Janice Joplin and the Grateful Dead used to hang out here, so I'd put that hammer away. No nails in her coffin just yet."

He was a feisty man with wild blond hair that could be best described as a Nordic Jew 'fro.

We sat down, and I immediately expressed my worries about getting the rights to do the play. I was concerned the publisher, or Jerry's estate, would sue us for using the book as our muse, and, in some instances, as our text. Stew gave me the contact info for Jerry's brother, who he believed was in charge of the estate, but told me not to bother with all that nonsense—it wasn't very Yippie like. Yippies didn't ask for permission to do things. Yippies just did them.

"What do you think would have happened if Abbie asked the New York Stock Exchange for permission to drop dollar bills onto the trading floor? Come on! The book is called *Do it!* Just do it. Listen, Randy, this country has got a real problem…"

I wondered to myself how many times he'd said that phrase. "This man that was just selected by the Supreme Court to be our President… This man is going to be real trouble. We all need to do everything we can to let people know that we the people are not going to sit back and watch our country be hijacked by this moron."

His energy and passion belied his years, and I feverishly wrote notes in my book. I kept asking pointed questions: Did you all become drunk with your own notoriety? Did you ever feel like ending the war was a lost cause? What was the point of trying to levitate the Pentagon? And in each instance, he answered the questions as simply as possible.

"Yes. No. The point was to call attention to the excessively bloated United States military machine."

And then, he would launch back into his fears about the growing strength of the religious right and the apathetic youth allowing it. He struck me as a little paranoid. But I suppose as a notorious activist during the '60s, his paranoia might have been justified. I wouldn't fully understand this until 2004 when I wrote a political comedy called *Kill the President* that we produced three blocks from Madison Square Garden during the Republican National Convention. Considering a lifetime of paranoia encouraged me to change the name of the play to *KtP*. As determined as I was to be a criminal, I was equally determined to remain on the outside.

Finally, Stew settled into telling some stories of the old days, which was the narrative I was after. For the next hour, I listened and wrote, laughed and learned. As we walked to the front door, Stew and Judy looked back into the deli and picked up whatever fragments of memories they could find in an old haunt clearly about to pass into history. I gave them both my card and promised I'd reach out with news of the show.

"Does this say *hog*?" Stew asked, as he stared at my business card.

"No, it says *TBG*. It's a lower case *t, b*, and *g*."

"Oh, I see. It looks like *hog*," he said to himself walking down the street.

"It's just a fucked-up font," I shouted into the six-story cannons of the Lower East Side.

Meeting with Stew illuminated how political the Yippies were. Like the hippies, they were masters of protest. We've all seen the pictures, massive crowds spilling across great green lawns framed by white neoclassical architecture. Hordes of angry people corralled behind police barricades with their fists in the air. We studied the faces of the discontent, read the signs they carried, and analyzed the anecdotes that served as captions. It must have been thrilling to be part of such a large and vocal opposition. We weren't aware then, but studying this history was preparing us for our own future movement.

Up until now, none of us had ever been to a real protest. To rectify this, all the *Do It!* creatives and my new boyfriend Scott got on a bus to Washington, DC, to protest the inauguration of George W. Bush, an election we all believed was stolen. We weren't quite ready to start dodging rubber bullets and sprinting through tear gas, so an organized and permitted protest seemed the safest way to initiate ourselves. George W. Bush would be inaugurated to the presidency, and we'd be inaugurated to protest. It was a big day for everyone.

During the whole trip down, Dickey and Harrison made fun of Scott and my kissy-kissy, cuddly behavior. And perhaps we were a little too cutesy, but I never got to be the one making out in the back of the high-school track bus, so I was making up for lost time.

When we arrived, Washington, DC, was cold and wet. We piled out of the bus, cloaked in winter coats and plastic ponchos, and assembled with our group. Despite the cold, we were excited. Something was going to happen today. We would make our voices heard. We took our signs out and began to march.

Now, we may not have known much about protests, but we could tell right away something was very wrong. First, our group leaders' order to stay on the sidewalk spread our group so thin we looked more like a parade. And then, the route raised questions. After 20 blocks of wondering through a quiet DC neighborhood, Dickey looked back and screamed, "Where the fuck are we?"

But his cry just echoed through the barren trees as we continued to follow a leader who was miles away for all we could tell.

"We know what democracy looks like! This is what democracy looks like!" we shouted. In this case, democracy looked like a tour group from Santa Fe gazing at DC architecture. Two by two, we wove through lettered streets like a kindergarten class utilizing the buddy system.

Finally, we arrived at the National Mall, a place we recognized, and we broke into a light jog over the damp grass. No longer tethered to the invisible rope of the group, we spread out over the vast green space, working our way toward the Washington Monument. The organizers shouted directions, but we knew our way to the Capital Building. We didn't need to be told what to do anymore; we were ready to fuck some shit up.

And then, not even halfway to the Washington Monument, we hit a fence. A serious fence. A huge 10-foot high, impossible-to-get-around fence. Is this it? Is this as far as we're going to get? We turned around to see the rest of our group talking to each other, trying to figure out what was going on.

It quickly became clear that this was where we were "permitted" to be, caged in somewhere behind the Washington Monument. We couldn't see the inauguration, we couldn't hear the inauguration, and, more importantly, those attending the inauguration couldn't see or hear us.

There were no spectators, no cameras, nothing at all. We were just a lonely band of 500 protestors, standing in the middle of the National Mall. Stew was right, we never should have asked for permission. Permits are for pussies. Protests happen when you're someplace you're not supposed to be.

I pulled Lolly aside. "We're not asking anyone for the rights. We're just going to do it." She nodded, and then dove into my arms for warmth.

"It's not like they're gonna kill us," she said. She was right. We'd already tangled with dangerous drug dealers. The worst thing a publisher could do is file a lawsuit, not a scary prospect when you have no money.

So, we began to take more risks—which, thanks to our newly created play development system, were nicely facilitated. At the start of each rehearsal, we'd place a bubble chart on the wall. This chart framed the points of the story we needed to hit, scene by scene. For each moment, someone would throw out an idea, and we'd improvise it. If the idea was good, we'd rehearse and refine it, and then move onto the next idea and then the next bubble.

Sometimes, the ideas were bad. In fact, at first, most of them were. But the more people stopped caring whether their ideas were good or bad, the more daring we got, and the more good ideas came out. After a few weeks, we finally arrived at a truly fearless rehearsal room, and the play started presenting itself through these collaborative improvisations. The less afraid you are to fail, the less you actually do fail.

By 4 p.m., we would finish the day exhilarated and exhausted. We'd pack up our props, someone would roll a joint, and we'd march from El Bohio through the East Village to the subway station. We quickly discovered that this march was one of our best marketing opportunities.

Selling an off-off Broadway show is a guerilla exercise, and our subject matter couldn't have been a better fit. The Yippies took their revolution to the streets, and so it was only fitting that we took our show to the streets. I'd attached two *Do It!* posters back-to-back on a stick to make what looked like a picket sign. Our image featured a shirtless Lolly with text obscuring her nipples, an army-issue combat helmet on her head, and her hand outstretched as if she were a traffic cop barking orders.

It was such a fantastic image I carried it around with me all the time. Everywhere I went—to and from Blah-Blah Big Bank, on the subway, in the park—I held this eye-catching image a foot above my head as if I had something to say. People noticed Lolly's screaming mouth and fleshy torso and would always look back to see if they had missed any actual nudity, which, of course, they hadn't. But it got their attention.

After rehearsal on weekend afternoons, when the East Village streets were full of people, we'd slowly wander down Eighth Street, passing a joint among ourselves and spreading ourselves out with the sign-carrier leading the way.

Timing was everything. People would see the sign, glance back for a second look, and someone would hand them a postcard. Just as they looked at the postcard, the unmistakable smell of marijuana would float past their nostrils. It was three-point advertising at its best. Point one, the sign piques their interest. Point two, they get the postcard with the information. Point three, the smell of pot attaches a memory to that postcard.

They'd put the postcard in their pocket and continue on with their day. When they got home, they'd empty their pockets, see the postcard again, remember the smell of pot, and maybe, just maybe, they'd make a point to come see what this show is all about.

Is that how it really worked? We'd never know. But it didn't matter. Selling the show was only part of what we were doing. New York, the land of concrete and steel, gets its color from the people on the street. That spring, the color was us. We loved giving those weekend-wanderers an East Village experience they would remember.

WITCHES' REVENGE

"All right, everyone! Let's get ready to do a run-through," I said walking out of the dressing room where Dickey and I had just jerry-rigged the smoke machine. It was the final week of rehearsals. We'd moved from our apocalyptic schoolhouse-come-rehearsal-hall into the musty den that was the Under St. Marks Theatre.

"Give us just a minute, I almost have it," Fanny said as she speared Nick's hand with a sharp metal object. Nick was playing John Doe, an impressionable youth who gets drawn into the revolution.

"You almost have what?" I asked, moving in for a closer look.

"Nick got a splinter. I'm taking it out."

"How did Nick get a splinter?"

"It's not really a splinter," Nick said, as he winced in pain. "It's like a rock or something."

"It's a pebble," Fanny corrected, and triumphantly held her tweezers in the air. "Got it!" she declared, and let out a high-pitched laugh.

"All right people, places!" I shouted.

We were at a turning point for the production. In the cycle of putting on a show, there is always a magical moment when you finally bring all the elements together. For this production, it wouldn't just be adding the lights and sound. This would be the first time we'd actually perform all the scenes in order. It would be the first time we'd see what we created. These moments can be disastrous or inspiring, and the only way to know which way it will go is to do it.

There are plenty of great characters in the play, from Jerry Rubin's high-strung communist Aunt Sadie, a character we made entirely out of clothing, to Sunny Tits, an undercover FBI agent who wears two-foot platform shoes, flower pasties on her bare chest, and a pistol in her crotch. But the real magic happens when Harrison, as the 1980s Jerry Rubin, begins a speech about returning to his London hostel on the Tube late one night in 1963 and noticing a headline on a fellow passenger's newspaper. Because the outside of the newspaper is upside-down, he, in true Yippie form, turns upside-down to read it. The headline announces the assassination of John F. Kennedy. As Harrison describes the scene, the rest of the cast creates a crowded subway car behind him. Jay, our guitarist, plays a haunting riff he had scored, and Tre Fleuve, our drummer, keeps time on his bongo as the cast performs synchronized headstands. Arms fall, heads lean to the side. We bend down, turn around. Heads hit the floor, and our feet turn skyward. We repeat this sequence throughout the speech and conclude with the creation of an upside-down JFK and

Jackie in the convertible waving to the crowd just moments before the shots ring out.

When we finished rehearsal, there wasn't an ounce of insecurity in the room. Everyone knew we'd created something special, and everyone knew they had a part in creating it. Two days before opening. One rehearsal left. We were certain to wow them on opening night.

I was sound asleep when my phone rang at 4 a.m. Looking back on events that woke me at 4 a.m., I can find only two. One was a call from my brother, who told me that my 17-year-old sister had given birth to a six-pound baby, when nobody even knew she was pregnant. And the other was in college when the 6.7 Northridge earthquake tossed me out of bed. So, my history of 4 a.m. wake-up calls literally consisted of one life and one death situation. Picking up the phone, I prayed for life.

"Hello?"

"Randy, it's Lolly. Nick's in the hospital."

Well... he wasn't having a baby.

"What? Why is he in the hospital? What happened?"

"I don't know. I just got off the phone... with him. He says it's bad? Something about...something about his arm or something?"

She was full of genuine drama. Not the artificial drama she usually possessed, but real life, situation-appropriate drama. This meant oddly placed pauses, fuzzy details, and inappropriate upward inflections, which made all her sentences sound like questions. I was going to have to get specific.

"Did he cut his hand on a bagel?"

"No! What are you talking about? A bagel?" I had obviously gotten too specific. But I couldn't imagine what might have transpired in the six hours since we last saw him. He seemed perfectly fine at rehearsal. "Well, what happened to his arm? Why did he call you?"

"I don't know. His friends have already been there? He says... I don't know, I didn't really understand. It's bad? Should we go down there? We should go down there right? I don't know, Randy. This is bad."

"Yes, we should. We don't know how bad it is yet. Let's go down there and find out. I'll get in a cab and pick you up."

I hung up the phone, threw on some pants and a sweatshirt, and headed to the street to catch a cab. I was still a bit hazy, but the more I woke up, the more active my imagination got. By the time the cab stopped to pick up Lolly, I had a whole scenario worked out.

"So listen," I started, as Lolly threw herself into the car, still dressed from the night before. She obviously wasn't in bed when she got the call. God, how I wished I was unemployed. "I bet he went out after rehearsal, because I think he said he was going to a bar with some friends, right? Didn't he invite Fanny? Did she go with him?" Lolly shook her head. "Anyway, I bet he got a little tipsy and, you know those stairs leading up to his apartment? They're real crooked like and narrow, and they have that door at the top. You know, the one with the stained glass." Lolly nodded, enraptured in my tale.

"Well, you know how it just sort of appears there, right?"

"No, I don't. Appears? What do you mean? The door is just there."

"Yes! It's just there. You know, there isn't a landing or anything. The door comes up to the lip of the stair. Like someone just put a door in the middle of a stairwell. Like it's not at the top of the stairs but sort of in the middle."

"Yes! I know what you're talking about. It's kind of weird."

"Very weird. So that's probably what happened." I finished, leaning back in the pleather, looking out the window. "I can never tell at this hour, if it's late at night or early in the morning."

"Um, are you gonna finish your theory? Or do you want to know the truth?"

"Do you know what happened?"

"No."

"Well..."

"So what does this door have to do with Nick's arm?" she asked.

I opened the window. I needed to cool my brain because it was overheating with all my imagining.

"It's simple. He got drunk and fell down his stairs. The door opens out over the stairs. It's a fucking disaster waiting to happen. It's hard enough to simultaneously open a door and climb stairs sober. I can't imagine trying to do that drunk."

"That's the dumbest thing I've ever heard, Randy. He goes into his apartment all the time. This can't be the first time someone's gotten drunk and opened that door."

"Well, do you have any better theories?" I asked, as the distinct smell of hospital filled the air.

"Randy, stop playing around. What are we going to do?"

"I don't know, Lolly, but it's 4:30 in the morning, and until we find out what's happening, I suggest we keep making up stories."

The cab pulled up to the emergency-room entrance, and we got out. I wasn't sure what we would say. If I can't visit a dying lover in the hospital, how was this going to play out? We couldn't ask to see him based on the fact he's in our play, could we? Luckily, we spotted him almost immediately in the hallway about 50 yards past the front desk. We walked in as if we worked there, and nobody stopped us.

"Nick, what the fuck happened?" Lolly asked, entirely too loudly.

"I can't move my arm," Nick replied. And indeed his arm was sort of propped up on the table next to him. Lolly gingerly poked at its flesh. "Don't ask me why they're making me sit in this wheelchair. I've been in it all night. Thanks for coming, you guys. You really didn't have to come down here."

He'd been crying and looked as if he was about to start again, which I didn't want to see and, I'm sure, he didn't want to do.

"We're concerned about you, Nick." I paused and took a breath. "So what happened? Besides you not being able to move your arm, does anyone know anything?"

"They think it's an infection. It started with my hand, and it's slowly been working its way up my arm. It's been the weirdest thing. I just slowly began losing the ability to move my arm. They've got me on some medication, and they think they've stopped it, but they're gonna keep me here for observation for a while longer."

This sounded bad, and suddenly the tears made sense. It wasn't physical pain, but rather a psychological torture he was enduring. I thought about asking him if it was permanent but decided against it. He probably didn't know, and that was probably what freaked him out the most.

"So, is this permanent?" Lolly asked. And sure enough, his eyes welled up. Most people have natural social filters that prevent them from saying everything that comes into their heads. Lolly's filters had been clogged for some time, so she'd had hers removed entirely.

"They don't know yet."

"Why do you have to go and ask such mean questions, Lolly?" I asked. She shrugged her shoulders and placed a comforting hand on Nick's shoulder. "So, how did you get this infection?"

"The only thing I can think of is the pebble that got wedged into my hand during rehearsal. It was either the pebble or Fannie's tweezers."

"It was the pebble," I said. "Fannie's tweezers are not going to have a super-bug living on them. It had to be the pebble."

And suddenly, my presence at the hospital shifted from concerned friend to liable employer. It wasn't like Nick was getting paid or anything, but still. I didn't ask, but I was certain Nick, like most other 20-something artists, did not have health insurance.

Thankfully, The Beggars Group has volunteer accident insurance, which is something every small theater company should have. I always thought it a bit ridiculous that we weren't paying people for their services, but we would spend all this money for insurance. Well, it wasn't so ridiculous anymore. But, like most insurance policies, it wasn't going to cover everything. We were bound to be on the hook for something. I immediately started calculating what all this was going to cost.

"Those god-damned fucking witches!" Lolly shouted. "I can't believe them."

Nick and I laughed uncomfortably while we looked around at the glances Lolly was getting.

"They put a spell on that pebble, you know. Back in the '70s. Back when that basement theater was their Wiccan meeting place. They probably did some ritual and put a spell on a knife or something, and some of the spell got onto this pebble that was then swept to the side, only to come out 20-some odd years later to infect Nick."

It was a fantastic, but not entirely implausible, explanation.

"Witches or rat poop," I said, as my calculations passed into quadruple digits.

"It was the witches, I'm telling you," Lolly repeated.

"Do you think they specifically targeted me, or am I collateral damage?" Nick asked. He was an improv guy after all.

"I don't know. Where were your parents in the '70s?" asked Lolly.

And they launched into a dialogue about Nick's fictional relations in the '70s. A corrupt politician, a prostitute, and a greedy accountant all made the short list of possible suspects who could have wronged the coven. This took our minds off the fact that half of Nick's torso was paralyzed until Lolly, laughing hysterically, threw her hand up to him for a high five. Nick looked at her hand, then at me, and thanked us for coming down. I promised him I would contact our insurance company, and we stepped out into the dewy spring air. It was now officially morning.

"We have to charge for the show," I said as we got into a cab.

"What? We can't. It's too late, Randy, we've been telling everyone it's free for weeks now," said Lolly, very sternly.

Several weeks back, Lolly and I made the very risky decision to not charge for tickets. We would forgo the traditional "buy your ticket, see a show" model and embrace the busker approach. Gather everyone around, do a show, and then ask for money. We were taking a gamble to get more butts in seats. And we were The

Beggars Group after all; so begging for money seemed appropriate. Somewhere in San Francisco, Aunt Phyllis was shaking her head. "I told you to call it The Emperors Group."

"This Nick thing could end up costing us a lot of money, and I'm not so sure we're going to make enough begging for tips."

Naturally, I was worried about killing the financial health of the company with this show. A feeling I'm sure every theater producer has on a daily basis.

"Well, we can't do anything about that any more," Lolly said. "It's done. We'll just have to wait and see."

"God, I wish we hadn't made that decision."

"It's done, Randy. We can't do anything about it now," Lolly said. I slumped into the seat and stared out the window. "What are we going to do, Randy?"

"About what?"

"About Nick! We open in two days!" I was silent for almost a minute. Lolly kept staring at me. "Randy, say something."

"Fucking witches," was all I could muster. It was their fault this happened. I hate witches.

When I got home, I showered, got dressed, and went to work. I picked up the phone and dialed.

"Noj, it's Randy."

"Hi, Randy," Noj replied.

"We have a bit of an issue."

"Oh, yeah, what's that?"

"Well, Nick hurt his arm, and we're going to need someone to step in for him."

"We open in two days!" he replied. I'd had this conversation before, only on the other side.

"Two days. That's right. Can you memorize lines quickly?"

"Yeah, lines shouldn't be a problem. Two days? That's fast..."

"Yeah," I said. Somehow, I knew he could do this. "I'm at work now, but Fannie, Lolly, and Dickey will be at my apartment all day. They'll teach you everything, and we have one more rehearsal in the theater, so you'll get a feel for everything."

"OK, I'm heading over there now," he said.

I hung up the phone and took a deep breath.

Nine hours later, when I arrived home, my apartment was buzzing with activity. Dickey was finishing props, Lolly and Fannie were synchronizing some dance steps I didn't recognize, and Noj was out on the fire escape screaming Nick's lines. Since he'd been running lights, he had a working knowledge of the staging. He only needed to tackle his lines.

"Anyone hear from Nick?" I asked, setting down my bag.

"He's gonna be fine," Lolly answered. "He's slowly starting to regain movement in his arm, and he should be 100 percent by next week."

What a relief. One week. We can make it through one week. Hell, the week will be easy if we could get through the next day.

"Why is he shouting?" I asked.

"He says it helps him to remember the lines," Fannie replied. "That's why we made him go outside. He was driving us all crazy in here. He's totally jacked up on Ritalin too. Do you want some?"

Everyone laughed except me. I didn't understand what was funny about being jacked up on Ritalin. I didn't even know what Ritalin was. I'd been to the doctor three times in the past 10 years. I didn't get sick and had, as of yet, no need for the pharmaceutical world. I just looked at them. I was too tired to even conjure a smile.

It was a very playful atmosphere that I truly wished I could enjoy, but I had a to-do list continually growing longer and more urgent, and I couldn't muster the strength for fun. I'd slept a total of six hours in the past 72, and our final rehearsal was the next day, followed by our opening that night. So, I calmly and quietly slipped into my bedroom, crawled into bed, and got to the business of sleep—the one thing on my to-do list that couldn't wait another moment.

GENTRIFUCKERS

Opening weekend came and went in a blur. We generated a great buzz, which resulted in mostly full houses. Reviewers were in and out, right along with the random folks we'd pulled from the street. By the time the second weekend rolled around, good reviews were in print, Nick was back in the show, and we were riding the wave of a hit. We were seeing the financial benefits as well. Each night, after the show, we'd give our speech to the audience.

"Thank you all for coming to see The Beggars Group's production of *Do It!* We hope you enjoyed yourselves. As a theater company, we strive to create a theatrical experience that inspires self-reflection, much as you might experience when passing a beggar on the street. But as we have a stage, lights, and costumes, we can do so in a far more entertaining fashion, hence the name The Beggars Group."

"Now, I'm sure you all noticed that you didn't pay anything when you came into the theater. That's because, as the Yippies would say, everyone should have free access to the theater. Actually, the Yippies would say that everyone should have free access to everything. But we'll only go so far as to let you into the show for free. But we do need your support. So, if you liked the show, on your way out, please drop some money into the hat. Shows like this usually cost between $10 and $20. If you really loved the show, by all means drop us a hundred. But, if you did not like the production and wish not to give any money, we only ask that you come up and tell one of us why. We won't bite. We want to learn. And if we're doing something that people don't enjoy, we want to know so we can do a better job next time. Thank you, and have a great night."

Everyone contributed. Even other poor young artists like ourselves dug into their pockets and found a few dollars, but most people contributed more. And by the second week, we were averaging almost $20 per person. The Beggars Group coffers were getting replenished and, thankfully, between Nick's insurance (that he actually did have, as it turns out) and our volunteer accident insurance, the hospital bills were paid. Everything was going our way.

The great thing about running a successful show is it creates a perpetual desire to celebrate. The show itself was a bit of a party, but afterwards we'd always find some kind of trouble to get into.

One night, we assembled at Harrison's apartment on 103rd Street to go, en masse, to a Gentrifucker party in Williamsburg. Nobody knew exactly who the Gentrifuckers were, or what they were about, but they sounded counterculture and hard-core, so we thought we'd check it out.

Our pre-party was in full force at Harrison's house when his partner burst through the door.

"Attention, everyone. May I have your attention?" The room quieted down. "I'm sorry to say that I won't be able to attend the Gentrifuckers party with you all this evening." He skipped introducing himself, as this was his house, even though he was among more strangers than friends. "But I have brought you a gift, given to me by my boss."

He pulled from a plastic grocery bag a square of foil, which he promptly began peeling open.

"Now, I know my boss's style, so I warn you all to proceed with caution."

He peeled back the last layer of foil to reveal a quarter-tray of brownies. The room erupted in shouts and applause.

I heard someone lean over to Fannie and ask, "Are those pot brownies?"

Fannie laughed. "Fuck, yeah!" And she pushed through the crowd, grabbed a square, and split it with her neighbor.

We devoured the delicacy in less than five minutes, and the room electrified with anticipation. For those of you who have never consumed marijuana in this manner, its effects take a good 45 minutes to an hour to present themselves. We all finished our beers before filing down the stairs and into the street.

While we were eager to meet the Gentrifuckers, we were primarily focused on being with each other.

Tonight, the journey was the destination. Armed with postcards and freed of our inhibitions, we piled onto the subway and slowly made our way downtown, bouncing around the train car with our fast and loud conversations. We had only two topics on our minds. What is this party going to look like? And when is the brownie going to kick in?

We emerged from the subway somewhere downtown to pick up our cast member Ria. Like Fannie, Ria was another "Daddy's little princess" whose lovability was so powerful, it managed to drag everyone miles out of our way so she wouldn't have to take the train to Brooklyn alone. Now, this wasn't Village downtown but Wall Street downtown—the downtown you seldom go to unless you work there, the downtown that on a Saturday night is all but deserted. We popped out of the subway hole in small groups, each moving a few feet from the stairs in different directions. We looked up at the towers around us and marveled at the empty quiet.

My gaze slowly floated down and landed on the reflection of our group in a storefront window. I was charmed by how young we appeared. We looked like children on the playground enjoying recess. And among our youthful chorus, I saw a beggar, larger in stature and much older, slowly approaching the group. I quickly turned around, but by the time I retrained my eyes from reflection onto reality, our group was all over the street in a chaotic wander and the beggar had vanished.

"Which way do we go?" I asked Fannie, who had been to Ria's house before. Fannie was in charge. She would be our guide.

"Um...I think it's this way," she said, lighting a cigarette and leading the group down an abandoned street. The mood of the group had shifted. We'd grown a little quieter. It was too early to tell whether this was a product of the brownie or just adaptation to our new environment.

"I don't like this," Dickey said. "Somebody is going to die."

"Don't say that!" Harrison said.

When Dickey said that, something bad usually *did* happen. It was his sixth sense. People wouldn't actually die, but something bad would surely happen.

"Great! You had to fucking jinx us, didn't you?" Lolly said. She knew. "Fannie, do you know where we're going?"

"It's down this way, I think."

"You think? Or you know?" Harrison shouted.

"I think. Stop worrying, you guys. We'll find it. God, just chill out and ride the brownie."

Ride the brownie. It was as if Fannie had thrown a match on us, and we were doused with gasoline. The laughter exploded over us like napalm. The brownie had arrived.

Other than the beggar apparition, we hadn't come across a single person since we'd emerged from the subway, and it felt as though we were walking in circles.

"We're walking in circles, Fannie!" Lolly said, not in a mad way, but as if she'd prefer to walk in squares. "You're taking us around in circles."

We turned down a very narrow street that curved to such a degree, you couldn't see the next intersection. This doesn't happen very often in grid of Manhattan, and we all pranced into the unknown with great delight.

Suddenly, a woman threw her body against the inside of a shop window. The fright nearly killed half our group. Screams were sent up through the canyons, followed by more laugher. It took what felt like an hour to collect ourselves.

Our first interaction with another human being was shocking enough. Like a caged lion, hungry for flesh, she'd thrown herself against this window. It was a tailor shop with floor-to-ceiling windows. Its light poured into the street. The youthful Chinese woman inside continued pounding on the glass and speaking a mumbled language I was certain none of us would understand. We approached with caution. Harrison took the lead.

"Are you OK?" he asked.

"Door no open! Door no open. Help!" she shouted.

Harrison stepped back to review the situation.

"It sounds like the door won't open, and she needs help," he said rubbing his head.

"Wow, Harrison, you're a fucking genius," Lolly said in her most sarcastic tone.

"Locked!" the woman shouted. "No key!"

"Oh, the door is locked, and you don't have the key!" Harrison replied to her, another outstanding deduction from our spokesperson. "How long have you been in there?"

It seemed like a silly question considering the circumstances until...

"Five hour! No people. Five hour! Please help!"

She hadn't seen anyone pass by for five hours? How was that possible? It was approaching midnight, but still, she must have seen someone. Something was getting lost in the translation. It was tragic that her only hope of rescue was a band of brownie-brained artists.

Finally, somebody had the presence of mind to get her to write down a phone number, which we promptly called from the one cellphone in the group. Why there wasn't a phone inside the shop was too difficult a topic to discuss. We notified the person on the line that someone they might know had been locked in a store for five hours, and if they would be so kind as to let someone else know, preferably someone with a key, we would be grateful. It was the best we could do without breaking the window, something we pondered, but decided against. We wished her luck and pressed on.

We finally found Ria's apartment and headed back to the subway. The topic of conversation revolved around how much we disliked downtown Manhattan with its sterile canyons of corporate office towers and flesh-eating tailor shops. But once the J train crept along the Williamsburg bridge, we pressed our faces against the windows, and all we could talk about was how beautiful downtown Manhattan looked and the dizzying heights of the skyscrapers reaching up, like flames, into the night sky. Some things just look better from a distance, like one's youth and mountains.

Halfway across the bridge, something else caught our attention. Dickey was turning green. And not green-*ish* or pale with a green hue, he was turning Shamrock Shake green.

"Dude, are you OK?" Harrison asked.

"No. No, I'm not feeling very good."

"I can tell. You're green."

"Shut up. Don't make fun of me. I really don't feel well."

"I know. You're green," Harrison repeated.

"That's not nice, Harrison," said Dickey, sweat building on his forehead. "I'm not feeling good."

Everyone saw what was coming and began to back away. Harrison stayed close and comforted him.

"I told you someone was going to die," Dickey said.

I looked over at Lolly. Could this be it? Was this going to be the first time someone actually died when Dickey said someone was going to die? The irony it would be Dickey was...terribly funny, and we couldn't help but laugh.

At least, that was what *I* was laughing at. No actual words were exchanged, so Lolly could have been laughing about something else entirely. And then the napalm hit again, and the whole subway car started laughing. Even people we didn't know—and who certainly hadn't shared our dessert—were laughing. It was a happy subway car. Everyone was happy.

Everyone except Dickey.

"I'm glad you guys are having a good time. You should have a good time. Don't be sad on my account."

It was an unfortunate thing for him to say. There is just nothing funnier than a martyr. So we laughed more.

Poor Dickey. It was terrible we were making fun of him. He'd been working his ass off hustling up quite a bit of money for the company. And I don't use those terms lightly. He was sleeping with the right people and managed to get our show seen by key foundation folks. Once they saw the show, we got the grants, but they probably wouldn't have seen the show had Dickey not lured them in. Morally questionable, yes... but oh so profitable.

Boy, was he turning green. It had progressed from Shamrock Shake to Incredible Hulk, minus the muscles. I didn't know people turned green. I turned yellow once when I had hepatitis, which seemed unnatural, but this green was otherworldly.

By the time we got to the first station in Brooklyn, Harrison had taken the address for the party and volunteered to accompany Dickey off the subway. The train doors opened, and Harrison expertly guided Dickey directly to the trashcan, where he began his business. The doors closed to the sounds of our fallen comrade, exorcising the brownie from his gut.

We finally arrived at the address listed on the Gentrifuckers' flyer. The neighborhood didn't look gentrified at all. It was half-industrial, half-residential, but there were no coffee shops, bars, or boutiques. No establishments you generally associate with gentrification. I began to wonder if these Gentrifuckers were so good at being against gentrification they'd managed to keep the gentrifiers away. We surrounded the large metal door and read the sign: "Don't knock, just kick the fucking door in." It was written with a Sharpie on white spiral-notebook paper.

After a brief conference, we decided to do what the sign said. So, I took a step away from the door, leaned back, and kicked the fucking door in. It flew open with such ease, it practically flew off its hinges. The half-dozen people sitting on the stairs on the other side practically wet their pants with fear.

"What the fuck are you doing?" one of the guys asked.

"The sign says, 'Kick the fucking door in,'" I replied as we began stepping over them. "Is the Gentrifuckers party upstairs?"

"Just 'cause the sign says...it doesn't mean...follow the music. You'll find it."

I wondered why he was so upset we'd kicked the door in. We couldn't have been the first people to follow instructions.

Once we got up the party, it became very clear we WERE the first people to "kick the fucking door in." The party was a bunch of Westchester kids slumming in Williamsburg in their pseudo-punk Gap clothes. The irony of the name Gentrifuckers was about as clever as this group got. We bounced around the party, joining conversations where we could, but nobody knew or cared much about gentrification, which was what we wanted to talk about. We couldn't find anyone who had any interest in social activism, so we looked for people who, at the very least, were as stoned as we were, but we couldn't find any of those either. Nobody was interested in talking to us about anything. It was a sad vibe.

Everyone there was so concerned about being part of a scene that nobody actually *was* a scene. I mean, who puts a sign on their door that says, "Don't knock, just kick the fucking door in," and then expects us to politely turn the handle?

Then, we learned that Gentrifuckers was the name of the band playing that night. This wasn't a group of activists after all. It was a party for a band with a name we mistook for a movement. So, we littered the place with postcards, filled up on keg beer, and left.

I imagine the next day, when they were cleaning up, the Gentrifuckers would wonder where all these postcards with the naked chick came from. Then, someone would stand up with his arms full of empties and say, "I remember them. They were the ones who kicked the fucking door in."

DOING IT ON YOUR BACK

At 6:30 p.m., I passed Tre Fleuve on my way into the theater. Our greeting was reduced to simultaneous nods of the head. My hands were full with two jugs of Carlo Rossini wine, and his were keeping the rhythm on his bongo drum. In the hour before our closing performance of *Do It!,* Tre Fleuve was busking up an audience.

"Free show! Free wine!" he shouted to the beat. "Come see us *Do It!* tonight at 8. Have some free wine that doesn't taste great."

We'd sweetened our free show "deal" by adding a little booze. Who was going to turn down a free show and free wine? Even those who had no intention of seeing a play that night could be drawn into our web. And if we got them a little sauced, they'd be more generous come tipping time. But Tre Fleuve wasn't kidding about the wine in his busking rhyme. It was God-awful.

Tre Fleuve's act started on the street as an innocent busking guy. But down in the theater, he became a whole different animal. We'd decided during rehearsals that Tre Fleuve and Jay should do some pre-show entertainment. They were, after all, musicians, and we thought it would be nice to have some ambient music while our audience choked down their fermented grape slurry, as they always did with great enthusiasm. We had no idea how this simple little idea would grow.

During their jam sessions, Tre Fleuve and Jay decided to become The Fucks. Not The Fugs, a favorite band of the Yippies. These alter egos were loud, offensive people and horrible musicians. The Fucks were not a band you wanted warming up your crowd. The Fucks were, to put it nicely, fucking fucks.

Every night, The Fucks brought a new surprise. Sometimes, they'd play a bad chord and recite dirty poetry until it stopped resonating. Other times, they'd scream at the audience about the injustices of caging a man's balls in tighty-whitey underwear. Or they'd make the audience participate in ridiculous games of call and response.

"When I sing 'douche,' you sing 'bag'!" Thankfully, most people paid little attention. They were too busy passing around the jug of wine.

We were not surprised when the reviewers showed no kindness to The Fucks. They always reserved a line or two to disparage our green show musicians.

"If you can get past the banality of the opening duo, who do everything in their power to make the audience leave, you will be treated to a fast-paced and inspired show. The Beggars Group would do well to cut them."

But we never did. That wouldn't be very Yippie-like.

"Can we open the house yet, Mr. Anderson?" Dickey asked, looking at his watch.

"In a minute," I replied.

"Is Scott coming?"

"He's in Italy already."

Scott had come to the show five times, and he really liked it, which relieved us both. He brought flowers and friends and quickly became a resident member of the *Do It!* family. His support was a blessing, and in one week, I would be joining him in Italy for a much-needed vacation after an exhausting six months.

Walking backstage, I told Harrison it was time for him to leave the theater. For Harrison's character, "places" meant wandering around the streets of the East Village until ten past 8. And, unlike everyone else in the show, he was dressed in a suit. He popped a chocolate into his mouth, and I followed him out. We emerged and exchanged "break-a-legs," as I watched him saunter into the twilight of East Eighth Street. I turned around and noticed a line forming. At the very front were my friends from Blah-Blah Big Bank, Rhonda and Roberta, munching on falafels. It was going to be a great closing night.

"We're going to open the house in just a few minutes," I told them.

"Don't worry about us," Rhonda said with her mouth half-full, holding up her dripping Middle Eastern snack. "We're having a great time already!"

Images like this stick out in my mind the most. Friends and strangers gathering for these short-lived pop-up communities is why I love doing all this work. I get such an electric charge out of bringing people together. I headed back into the theater, two steps at a time. We had to open the house immediately. The tattoo parlor next to the theater doesn't take kindly to people blocking their stoop—and tattoo people are not the kind of people you want to piss off.

"House is open!" I shouted while doing a quick sweep of the space.

I poked my head out onto the street, informed Rhonda and Roberta the house was open, and they got the line moving. As the audience entered, Ria handed them a manila folder marked "Confidential." This dossier contained everything the audience needed to know about the Yippies, Jerry Rubin, and The Beggars Group. That's far more reading content than usual for a production of this scale, but we were inspired by the edifying programs you could purchase at a West End production and wanted to re-create that experience.

The Fucks played some ambient music that actually sounded good and left the audience to pass that big jug of wine back, aisle by aisle. The rest of the cast milled about the stage waiting for The Fucks to make their move. And sure enough, they stopped playing, and Jay welcomed everyone to the closing night of *Do It!,* which was greeted with applause. "Don't encourage them!" I thought.

He then invited the audience on stage for a dance party. A dance party! The lights came down, funky dance music blasted over the speakers, and within minutes, the whole audience was on stage, jumping and twisting. Jay and Tre Fleuve passed through the crowd, bouncing and gyrating. And then I saw him. It was C.J., hopping through the group with that adorable grin.

A whole series of emotions flew through me, but the one that stood out the most was judgment. I felt judged. He didn't approach me, though I was sure he saw me. He probably hadn't anticipated dancing with the performers prior to the show. I watched him for a minute and allowed myself to feel everything one feels when seeing an old love for the first time in over a year.

It took a moment to get over the fear of feeling so much, but when I did, I realized this judgment wasn't coming from him. It was coming from me. He just came to the show, most likely, to be supportive of my endeavors. To be supportive of me! And like everyone else, he didn't come expecting to see something bad. He didn't come to judge. He showed up with the hopes of seeing something good. And if I was proud of this show, why wouldn't he be?

And suddenly, because sometimes in life things happen suddenly, I was able to forgive myself. Until that moment, I wasn't aware this was something I needed to do. I hadn't realized the tremendous blame I put on myself for having "failed" a relationship. But now, I could forgive myself, learn from it, and move on. In fact, my relationship with Scott had demonstrated I already had. The second I did that, I felt wonderful. Judgment turned to joy, and I was glad C.J. came and looked forward to catching up with him after the show.

The song ended. The audience applauded and returned to their seats and their wine. The Fucks, for the first time during the run, actually performed the task they were given: warm up the crowd, which they had done quite literally. Our audience was now sweating profusely and fanning themselves with their dossiers.

Harrison burst into the theater. "Sorry I'm late," he announces to the audience in a formal tone. "Welcome to the seminar on *Do It!*"

And the play begins, inside a seminar led by Jerry Rubin from the 1980s. Jerry, like many other 1960s radicals, turned from Yippie to Yuppie during the Reagan years. He dabbled in the world of est, got involved with pyramid schemes, and engaged in other suspect business endeavors. *Do It!* features this 1980s Jerry confronting his past, a past materializing behind him as he waxes on about memories.

"When I think about my past..." our Jerry continues.

Behind the spread-out white sheet hanging over the backstage door, the shadows of the '60s grow in size and in volume. Smoke spills out from the back and, just as the amplification of the past overtakes the sounds of the present, the sheet drops to reveal the Chicago Riots. Smoke and screams fill the room and then stop in an instant as the focus falls on young Jerry, played by me. I hold an army-issue gas mask as if it were a pig's head.

Raising a knife into the air, I shout, "I'm gonna do it! I'm gonna kill this fucking pig."

Then, silence. The stage falls into order, and we flash back to where it all started, the 1950s.

About 20 minutes into the hour-long play, we come to a scene called "Troop Trains." The Yippies attempted, with their bodies, to stop trains from transporting U.S. soldiers through Berkeley. While their second attempt was successful, the first was not, and we staged both scenes in slow motion. The light of the train engine moves across the stage toward our crowd of Yippies, who throw their arms in the air and shout in silence. As the train moves through the group, we lift a few performers by their feet and turn them upside-down to create the illusion of leaping bodies.

As I am about to lift Nick, he bends down and places his hands on the stage. I squat, grab his feet, and start to stand up. Then, I feel something slip. Not on the floor. Not off my body. It's something *in* my body, something in my lower back. It doesn't hurt at first, but suddenly, I can't support my own weight, let alone Nick's. I promptly drop him on the floor, which temporarily ruins the illusion of the slow-motion troop-train dodge.

Something terrible has happened, and I have no idea what. We still have another 40 minutes of show, and the pain I didn't experience at first begins to make its presence known. Still ahead, I'm to perform a song-and-dance number that includes several group lifts and a long list of other highly physical feats.

This includes Fannie jumping on me and wrapping her legs around me as I gyrate my hips, simulating intercourse. I also leapfrog over some folks, lie on my belly, push backwards on the floor, get up and leapfrog again to simulate an advancing protest line. Thankfully, I only stand still for the courtroom scene. And then, I'm set to perform 12 headstands in the JFK assassination scene. In the finale, Harrison (with gas mask on) will wrap himself around my waist. I lift him in slow motion, and, while he's still holding my waist, his entire body jets out to the side and turns upside-down before settling back around my waist and, in a full body C-clamp position, assumes the role of the pig I am about to kill at the beginning. No wonder my back just exploded.

I know I can't make it. But at this moment, I am dripping in the wonder drug called adrenaline, so I press on. I fudge my way through the song and let the others do the brunt of the lifting. I manage to hold Fannie long enough to simulate teenage-boy sex (two thrusts), which she plays off of brilliantly. My leapfrogs turn into rollovers. The headstands actually feel pretty good. It's no picnic coming out of it, but once there, I get a brief reprieve from the rapidly increasing pain. I've almost made it to the end and can hardly wait to lie down. I only have to get past the "pig" bit.

Harrison and I square off. I'm sure everyone notices something is not quite right, but like me, they have no idea how bad my injury is. Standing there, looking at 175 pounds of muscle and bone, I realize that somebody will die if I try this lift. I start shaking my head.

By the look of sheer terror on my face, Harrison knows he's on his own. So, he makes up some tumble movements while I stand by and watch.

Once the show ends, I run to the dressing room and lie flat on my back. There I stay, through the curtain call, the closing speech, and the dispersing of the audience. I then try to sit up but realize that isn't going to happen. While the cast packs up around me, Dickey calls for help.

Within minutes, the paramedics burst through the door. These two good-looking men in their 20s, dressed in paramedic outfits, seemed like they just walked out of a hunky calendar. After assessing my situation, in a hot second they offered me two choices. They could help me up, give me some aspirin, and put me in a cab, or they could help me up, put me in the ambulance, and take me to the hospital, which would cost a great deal more.

"So, basically, what you're saying is that I have to get up," I said.

"Yes," said Hot Paramedic Number One. "You have to get up."

"Well, how am I going to do that?" I asked, staring into his hot paramedic eyes.

"Grab our arms, and we'll pull you up," replied Hot Paramedic Number Two.

"Just like that?"

"Just like that."

The idea I would get to touch not one but two hot paramedics was so thrilling, I almost forgot how painful the maneuver would be. Is that why they send the attractive paramedics to calls like this? I wouldn't have been able to do it if they were what my former agent Patty called "normal-looking."

"Come on," said Hot Paramedic Number Two. "You don't have a choice. You gotta just do it."

"*You* fucking do it if it's so easy," I wanted to say, but I didn't want to jeopardize the imaginary three-way I'd be having with them in the ambulance.

Scott wouldn't mind, would he? After all, how often do two impossibly hunky paramedics come along to rescue you? I grabbed their arms, and in one painfully awful move, they pulled me up to stand. I draped my arms over their shoulders, and they escorted me to the street.

Opting to save a few thousand dollars, I got into a cab with Lolly and Nick and, feeling helpless and overwhelmed, immediately started to fight back the tears. It wasn't so much the pain. It was the idea that this could be permanent. I looked at Nick, who put his hand on my shoulder. He knew exactly how I felt.

Back at the apartment, where our cast party was underway, I rolled around on an exercise ball, and Big Rob burst into the apartment with cigars.

"Congratulate me! I'm gonna be a dad!" he bellowed and looked down at me. "What happened to you?"

"I threw out my back. Did you just have a baby?"

"No, but my girlfriend is pregnant. I'm gonna be a daddy! Tee-hee."

Big Rob "tee-hees" a lot. It's his favorite expression. He is the only person I know who actually verbalizes it, but having a baby seemed to warrant more than just a tee-hee. He'd been dating a girl in California for a while, and, apparently, one of his brief visits had made a baby. I guess that's what happens when you mess around with real vaginas.

"You know, you're not actually supposed to break out the cigars until the baby is born," I said.

"I know," Big Rob replied. "But I'm happy. And I like smoking cigars. So fuck it! Let's smoke."

A few weeks later, he'd be gone. He'd had his New York adventure, and now it was time to settle down. With his departure, I began to realize the transient nature of New York. As a professor once told me, New York is a great place to be rich and a great place to be young. And over the years, I've seen a lot of people "age out" of the city, usually, when a baby's on the way.

The next day, I managed to get to the doctor and begged, not for pain medication, but for something to speed my recovery. I'd only been to see Dr. Kline once before, but I think he already had me figured out. When I'm with medical professionals of any kind, I tend to talk nonstop. It's my whole, "get therapy wherever you can" philosophy.

So, I treated Dr. Kline to a full description of how I was about to embark on a wildly romantic trip through Italy, and I needed to be well enough to go. Scott and my relationship had survived those five months, and I couldn't just let my body ruin this trip. I didn't care how much it hurt; I just wanted to walk. I'd worked hard. I was falling in love. I had to get to Italy. After about five minutes of my babbling, Dr. Kline said he could treat me like a cheating athlete and give me some steroids.

"Does that show up on drug tests? 'Cause my work sometimes tests for drugs." I was oddly more concerned about doctor-prescribed steroids than all the pot I'd been smoking.

"Unless you're planning on competing in an athletic event, which I don't recommend in your state, I think you'll be fine," he said, showing me the door.

I spent most of the 12-hour journey fondly reflecting on the past several years. The company had grown considerably, but more importantly, I had grown considerably. And I could feel another one of life's shifts coming. I had no way of knowing what shape it would take, but my first clue came when I arrived in Italy. After several dizzying transfers from planes to trains to cabs, I found myself safely in Scott's Bologna hotel room. With Scott still at work, I crawled right into bed and quickly fell asleep at one in the afternoon. Six hours later, I opened my eyes to find Scott quietly reading in bed next to me.

"You have perfect timing," he said, as he closed his book, ready to go out for dinner.

But to me, his comment meant far more than my awaking in time to eat. After fumbling with my emotional availability for most of my adult life, I'd started to grasp the need to express myself in a different way, to allow myself to love and be loved, not in the past and not in the future but in the present. And while I couldn't fully agree with the perfect part, my timing *was* getting better, which was fortuitous because, once again, I was falling in love.

Part V
STOPPING THE WORLD

ALL ABOUT THE SPACE

"So, what's next for you guys?" Beverly asked as we piled a second helping of pulled pork and fried okra onto our plates.

"*Stopping the World*," I said. "An exploration of the profound moments that forever alter our perception of reality."

We were still working on the tagline and in no way prepared to give a description, so I got off the subject.

"You have a beautiful home, Beverly. Thanks again for putting this together for us. We haven't eaten this well all week. I guess this is what they call southern hospitality."

Beverly, who is cast-member Kevin's mom, had invited the *Do It!* cast to her home for some southern barbecue to celebrate the completion of our week in Atlanta.

Noj's brother, Chris, and another Moon Monk ran an Atlanta art gallery/event space called Blue Milk, and they invited us down to perform *Do It!* Eager to go out on the road, we flew 12 people south for a one-week run. A whole week without day jobs or city distractions meant we could accomplish a lot. We'd do four *Do It!* performances, a more coherent musical staging of Noj's *Odd-Eye-See* (yes, another *Portal Opening*), and a series of daylong workshops to explore the aesthetics of our next production, *Stopping The World,* which we'd present at FringeNYC the following month.

"What exactly do you mean by *Stopping the World*?" Beverly asked. "I don't quite understand."

Southerners like to talk, so I wasn't going to get away with just the title and the tagline. I grabbed another beer, which Beverly reflexively opened, and we walked out into the steamy July heat, where some of the boys were engaged in a friendly but physical game of basketball.

"The idea comes from Carlos Castaneda's book, *Journey to Ixtlan,*" I started, as we sat on wooden deck chairs. "In the book, Castaneda speaks of the need to stop the world in order to begin 'seeing.' For his character, Don Juan, this was something he actively tried to do, but for the purposes of our show, we want to explore what happens when a stopping-the-world moment happens to you when you're not looking for it."

"That's the part I don't understand. What's a stopping-the-world moment?" Beverly asked.

We'd been entrenched in the subject all week, and formulating the concepts into a few sentences still proved very difficult. I needed Andrea's precision smarts.

"We want to investigate..." That was the wrong direction. "What we're exploring are those profound moments when your world stops, you know? When you're forced to 'see' differently. A paradigm shift."

I was getting closer.

"And we're looking at it from two perspectives—the personal level, like the death or a birth of a loved one, and the universal level, when we collectively experience a paradigm shift, like the dropping of the atomic bomb or say...an alien invasion."

"That sounds very dramatic."

"Exactly! They're the most dramatic moments in our lives. Once a 'stopping-the-world moment' happens to you, the way you perceive the world is changed forever. Going back to your old way of thinking is an almost impossible task."

"Well, if you do as good a job as you did with *Do It!,* I'm sure it will be great." She stood to continue her hostess duties, and I put my feet up and watched the game.

We had a lot to celebrate. The final Atlanta performance of *Do It!* was a magical experience for performers and viewers alike. We transformed one of the gallery rooms into an intimate venue, where the audience sat all around us on couches and beanbags. It's best described as living-room theater. One of the best things about live performance is that it can happen anywhere—and often improves outside the confines of a traditional theater. This downtown gallery den was one of those special places, in direct contrast to where we'd been only a month earlier.

Upon my return from Italy and in preparation for our Atlanta presentation, Dickey found us free rehearsal and performance space in Long Island City, Queens. This entire second floor of a large warehouse building, not far from the Queensborough Bridge, was simply called The Space. The woman responsible for running The Space worked for a local politician whose campaign office was on the first floor. The exact nature of their relationship was suspicious, but getting embroiled in a political scandal seemed a small price to pay for a free place to work.

With its maze-like floor plan, giant industrial windows, bare walls, and cement floors, The Space was "Soho chic" in Queens. Several of the rooms already operated as art studios, and one room, right in the middle, was established as the theater.

After three solid days of work, we had cleared out and created the performance space. This huge room had an elevated stage that measured 50 feet across and 30 feet deep. Since we had no official ties to The Space, we weren't going to spend any money on the renovations, so we had to rely on the resources immediately available, which limited the possibilities.

Then, we discovered the Magic Room, buried deep at the far end of the floor. This large storage room contained piles and piles of junk the visual artists would disappear into when they were looking for materials. As we cleared out our room, we'd make ridiculous requests of the universe and then send someone into the Magic Room to see if we were heard.

"Wouldn't it be nice if we could have nice movie-theater seats for the audience?" Dickey pondered, as he swept up five inches of dust.

Harrison and Lolly entered the Magic Room and came back pulling the first few of 30 movie-theater seats behind them.

"The room is too big. I really wish we had giant black curtains to cut the space in half," Harrison entreated, as he fixed a loose corner of the stage deck. Thirty minutes later, a team appeared dragging giant asbestos-soaked black curtains behind them.

We continued to make such magical discoveries all week. We found clip lights, rope, red curtains, Masonite, everything you needed to make a theater. Yes, we're a sharp bunch, but for some reason, it took us the whole week to realize this space actually *was* a former theater that had been taken apart piece-by-piece and put into the storage room. We simply put it back together.

"We just re-created the wheel!" I exclaimed.

Only Lolly laughed. We got so caught up in the act of re-creating the wheel, we didn't even know we were doing it. Somewhere, Andrea was laughing at us.

After we had reconstructed the theater, we began reconstructing *Do It!* Harrison and I swapped roles—with me as the less physical 1980s Jerry and him playing the hyperphysical 1960s Jerry—and Lolly started stripping the script down to its bones. Tre Fleuve put together a new band, complete with electric guitar and bass.

Our group hotly debated the merits of reconstructing, as opposed to re-creating, the show. Even today, I'm not sure where I stand on the topic. To adapt the show to this new space, some changes were necessary; but our full-scale demolition put the baby on its ass in the gutter.

That was only the beginning of our troubles. Rooms have energy, as any architect or interior designer will tell you, and this room—in fact, the entire building— brimmed with anger. And it wasn't just the post-war design or the bland concrete coffin-esque shape of the rooms.

Whatever happened there in the past 50 years was not good. I don't know if this building housed an illegal drug operation or an illegal sweatshop, but right when we started rehearsals, fights broke out. We weren't agreeing on *anything*, and no one was being nice about it. The space was Yoko Ono-ing us. Our Yippie revolution turned into cast-mate revulsion. Everything sucked. The band was too loud, the script was too mangled, and the performances were too forced. We had consumed every last bit of Yippie fun and shat it all over the stage.

By the third time we presented this lousy, angry production to equally lousy, angry audiences, everyone was ready to push each other off the Queensborough Bridge. The Space had possessed us and was sucking our artistry right out of our bones. Perhaps the politician and his questionable employee lured artists into The Space to suck out their creativity and collect it in Mason jars for future campaign speeches.

We'd never know because, by the time we started conjuring conspiracy theories, it was too late. We had this mangled shred of an angry show to pack into our suitcases and bring down to the fine folks of Atlanta.

As excited as we were for our adventure, I was panicked about the state of our affairs. We had mapped out almost every minute of every day, but we still had a lot of unknowns—chiefly, the space. An oversized art gallery in Queens had just eaten us alive, and now we were heading down to Atlanta to spend an entire week in yet another art gallery.

From the moment we arrived, we attacked the schedule with military precision. Workshops began promptly at 9 a.m. Breaks occurred regularly at an allotted time, and everyone remained focused on the task at hand. We were running a theatrical boot camp, which worked well...for a day and a half.

"Goddamn it! I fucking quit!" Dickey slammed his fist on a Styrofoam container, sending a mix of mashed potatoes and coleslaw flying in every direction.

Lolly, not holding back, laughed in his face. It's a particular kind of viciousness I'm convinced she can't control.

"Calm down, Dickey," I said. "Nobody is quitting."

Our midday lunch meeting at a fast-food chicken joint had gone south when Lolly started antagonizing Dickey about the way he represented the company.

"He can quit if he wants to," Lolly said. "If he's going to keep goofing off during workshops, I think he should quit."

Dickey's face and cleanly shaved head were as red as a radish. His ability to change colors amazed me.

"I was having fun, Lolly!" Dickey shouted. "What's wrong with having a little fun? And yes, Randy, I quit. I'll stay for the rest of the trip, but when we get back, I'm done. I'm not working with this bitch anymore."

He got up and walked out the door, leaving his mashed-potato mess behind.

"Can you believe him?" Lolly asked, laughing a little. "Am I wrong?"

We sat in silence. She was wrong. She shouldn't have antagonized him that way. But Dickey knew Lolly was provocative. He never should have let her get to him like that. Once Lolly gets to someone, she doesn't hold back. But boy was she behaving badly.

"Lolly," I said. "You have to stop pissing people off!"

"What are you talking about? They're pissing *me* off!"

"Maybe he's right. Maybe we need to relax a little."

"We can relax, Randy, but he was being downright childish. I expect more from a company member."

I think she was exaggerating about Dickey. He and Fannie giggled a lot during the movement workshop, but I think that was largely because Fannie moves so well and Dickey does...not.

"Well, then, you're going to have to figure out a better way to get it," I said.

Lolly just huffed.

"Look," I said, as I mopped up Dickey's mashed-potato mess. "This isn't working. We have to find a better way to, I don't know, get everyone engaged."

"They'd *be* engaged if they didn't see a core company member fucking around. He's not trying, Randy."

I bent over to wipe up some coleslaw and simultaneously hide the rolling of my eyes.

"Now, why do I feel like I've heard that before?" I asked.

"Probably because you have. I don't want to work with people who aren't giving 100 percent to this company."

I'd run out of napkins and needed to make a trip to the condiment station.

"We're the only people who are going to give 100 percent, 100 percent of the time, Lolly. That's kind of how it's always been. We can get people to give 100 percent, but we have to decide when we want them to do that, and then give them some downtime."

I had only just figured that out as I was saying it. And it made so much sense. We sat in silence for a moment, processing.

"Will you please go make things right with Dickey?" I asked, walking toward the counter.

"Fine," she said as she walked out, leaving me the mess and another real-life-as-metaphor moment.

Our intense drive to make things happen was hindering the act of actually making things happen. And in fighting so hard to not repeat the angry Queens production, we had lost track of how to create the kind of production we actually wanted. We desperately needed a shot of creativity.

Enter the Prudenians.

That evening, after we all ate dinner, we lined up outside a broom closet to open the portal. The idea was to enter the closet as an earthling, sit for a minute, and then emerge as a Prudenian. I watched the first few people walk in as if they were casting themselves into a volcano. Then, they came out as a Prudenian, introduced themselves to everyone, and behaved more childlike than alien-like. This did nothing to ease the skepticism I had during the *Portal Opening* in New York, but this time I couldn't hide in the tech booth. The company was starting to fracture again, and Prudenia was the new Fire-Food. So, I stepped into the closet, and a Moon Monk closed the door behind me.

I sat there in the darkness, thinking about the week, the production, the budget, Scott...but not about my Prudenian. Finally, after what felt like eternity, someone opened the door.

"Hello!" Blue said. "Who are you?"

It was as if I were sitting on the toilet with everyone looking at me. I was completely caught off guard.

"Hello everyone," I started. "I'm Knick-owww."

It wasn't a name, really. It was a click of the tongue followed by an *owww*.

"Hello, Knick-owww," Blue said without missing a beat. "Welcome to Earth. Everyone, this is Knick-owww." His pronunciation of my made up name was astounding.

He led me into a group of people I already knew but seemed unfamiliar—Fierce Grape, Sapphire, King Telemachus. The names were all out of this world and much easier to pronounce than my own. But now that I was one of them, I released my judgment and began behaving more freely. And everyone else did, too. Lolly and Dickey's differences vaporized. Judgment died, and creativity soared. We lunged straight into rehearsals for *Odd-Eye-See* and built a more structured but still freeform musical interpretation of Homer's epic poem.

We closed the portal several hours later by individually entering the broom closet, sitting there for a moment, and returning as ourselves. But we never fully came back. Sure, we called each other by our given names and maybe didn't act quite so goofy, but we maintained that childlike freedom I'd been mocking earlier. That creative freedom, woven into our overly structured week, generated an artistic force you'll often find in an art camp.

We reconfigured our performing space, re-adapted the *Do It!* script, and rehearsed into the morning's wee hours. Tre Fleuve's band and the actors fell into perfect sync. When we presented our production for 30 people in that red-walled gallery, the energy rang out like a tuning fork—smooth, consistent, and with perfect pitch. The color, flavor, and texture of the show were perfect. We all felt it. This was The Beggars Group's ripest moment.

The basketball game had ended, and we all congregated on the court, alternatively passing around a bottle of Jack and a joint.

"Thank you, guys, for a great week," I said to the Moon Monks.

"No, thank *you*," Chris replied. "You guys brought so much energy and excitement. This has been an incredible week. Really inspiring. Here, here!"

We raised our glasses just as Beverly poked her head through the door.

"There's so much food left. I want each and every one of you to come up here and make another plate."

Beverly had perfect timing. The munchies were just starting to hit.

FAG HOG

"You guys," Dickey started, as we walked down Stanton Street in a blazing August heat. "We have to stop this…"

Lolly and I both knew what he was going to say next.

"…or somebody is going to die," we said together.

He was right, but the situation was out of our hands. We couldn't do anything about it now, could we? We could have done something a few days ago, but now? How could we let this happen? More to the point, how could we stand by and let it get worse? Because it *was* going to get worse. That much we knew.

It all started when we got back from Atlanta. Or maybe it started when Dickey picked that horrible font for our cards. Who knows when these things start? Does anyone really know when the insidious crack forms on the dam? Our crack was forming. That much we knew.

We had pulled together plenty of fantastic ideas for our new show, *Stopping the World*, in Atlanta, but we only had two weeks until our first performance at FringeNYC. Two weeks, and we didn't have postcards, posters, flyers, or even a show. All we had was our concept. And the title! We had the title. We had a concept and a title. We'd gotten by with less, hadn't we? Surely, we could put something together with sheer determination and a little luck, right? After all, we created the TBG Development System.

We spent Week One mapping out a basic structure by combining Shakespeare's stages-of-man speech from *As You Like It* with a brief history of evolution. This would illustrate the personal and the universal. The idea was to establish the growth of a human being and the evolution of life on the planet. Once the audience identified the pattern, they'd begin predicting the next steps. After all, they're fairly predictable to everyone—everyone except creationists, I suppose, but creationists don't often attend fringe theater festivals. Then, once the audience was comfortable, we'd introduce a "stopping-the-world" moment. We'd interrupt this predictable path with some tremendous event. We got to work piecing together the script, using the Bard and Darwin texts as our references.

During Week Two, we were allowed into the theater to start rehearsals. We arrived at Fringe Central on Stanton Street on the Lower East Side. While we weren't expecting much from our facilities, we thought, at the very least, we would have four walls.

Unfortunately, that wasn't the case. We were placed in what we referred to as "Afterthought Theater." With a corrugated tin roof and tent walls, it was the shantytown venue of the festival, the theater that had to be built when the organizers realized they didn't have enough space for all the shows they'd accepted.

The one benefit to performing in Afterthought Theater was its location in Fringe Central, the festival's hub of activity. Not only was this where people bought their tickets for the shows, it was also where performers and patrons mingled, which generated numerous marketing opportunities.

Of course, the crappy venue was the least of our worries. We still needed to come up with a show. When we got into the space, Lolly and I decided to illustrate the evolution of man and mankind not only through our actions and words but also through the audience. If you're weak on content, make it interactive! The audience would begin watching the show from the stage floor while lying on their backs. Then, we'd ask them to sit up to watch from their bums. Next, they'd stand for a period, and, after five more minutes, we'd lead them to their seats, where they would remain fully evolved audience members for the duration of the show.

In two weeks, that was as far as we got. We had woven together 30 minutes of found text, an accompanying series of highly physical actions, and an evolving audience experience. All of this led to the big "stopping-the-world" moment—a moment that didn't exist. Mere hours before our first show, we'd only managed to generate the first half. It was a good first half, but it was only a half.

"We're so screwed!" Lolly said in a complete panic she covered by laughter.

"Yeah, yeah, we are," I said. "I mean, I guess we just do the show until we don't have a show and then stop. We can explain to the audience that it's a work in progress, and, if they want to see the rest, they should come back toward the end of the festival. Maybe we could use it to our advantage and get some repeat customers."

It was foolishly optimistic for sure.

"Nobody is coming back, Randy," Lolly said. "Would you go back to a show like that?"

"Maybe," I replied.

"No, you wouldn't."

She was right.

"I've got it," said Dickey, pointing his finger to the heavens.

Lolly and I recognized instantly that Dickey was about to make some crazy joke, and she cut him off at the pass.

"Dickey, we need to be serious right now. We have to figure this out."

"Or," Dickey countered back, "we aren't serious." He grinned mischievously. "What if we do the show up to the point where we don't have a show, and then the lights mysteriously go out? There is some commotion, a loud noise, and when the lights come back on, we're gone."

A really bad magic trick! Sadly, it was the best idea yet, but it seemed incomplete.

"Where did we go?" Lolly asked.

"Fag Hog took you," Dickey said.

Lolly and I exchanged a look. Because of Dickey's poorly chosen font, people constantly thought the *tbg* on our stationery and business cards said either "fag" or "hog," depending on their particular level of crassness. And that was how the myth was born.

We'd been working on the legend of Fag Hog for almost a year. Fag Hog was an irresponsible band of fucked-up theater makers. A short brush with The Beggars Group had made them lifelong enemies. Their logo was a well-chosen font that said both "fag" and "hog" at the same time, utilizing only three letters. Sadly, this ingenious logo was often confused with the better-known Beggars Group, whose logo was quite similar. Fag Hog didn't just make bad theater, they made bad human beings. The thought of conjuring their presence now was dangerous and thrilling.

"Yes," Lolly said. "And then we come out as Fag Hog and terrorize the audience."

Lolly and I started laughing. It was a ridiculous idea we never should have followed through with, but possessed by panic and inspired by necessity, we did. In a matter of minutes we had assembled costumes and props that consisted of a sombrero, ponchos, swimming goggles, a bag of flour (that would represent cocaine), a bottle of tequila, and a stage gun. We headed down to the theater.

Our first audience is light, which isn't surprising since we hadn't advertised. We pull in our venue manager, Dom, to help fill out the seven-person audience, and the show begins.

At first, nobody knows what to make of being instructed to lie on the stage, but once we start running in place and vibrating the floor, everyone gets it. This is the massaging portion of the show. Since the novelty of watching a show from your back wanes quickly, we easefully move the audience from lying positions to sitting. We get them up to sitting, then standing, all the while telling the magical stories of the growth of humanity.

Right as we run out of play to perform, the lights go out. Lolly and I yell and hit things backstage while we change into our Fag Hog costumes. Thirty seconds later, the lights come back on, and we burst onstage complete with ponchos, booze, swimming goggles, "cocaine," and toy guns.

"Fuck The Beggars Group!" Lolly shouts. "We're Fag Hog, and we're gonna show you what real theater is!"

This commences our improvised disparaging of The Beggars Group.

"Ladies and gentleman, what you've been witnessing here is complete crap!" I explain. "The Beggars Group likes to claim they make good theater. But they don't! We do!"

"Yeah, we do!" Lolly chimes in. "We make good theater. We just can't...well, we just don't have anything...theatrical, I mean, that we can do right now."

"That's not true," I say.

And we launch into a really bad series of improvised skits. When I say "bad," I mean really, really, REALLY bad. Once we finish (a merciful five minutes later), Dickey brings the lights back down, and we noisily change back into Randy and Lolly. The lights return, and we walk, half-dazed, onto the stage.

"Ladies and gentleman, we apologize for the interruption," I announce. "I don't know what to say. Those people are awful. They answered an ad we placed in the *Village Voice* looking for collaborators for this festival..."

"Obviously," Lolly continues, "these are not the kinds of people we want to get involved with." She is on the verge of tears.

"We'd like to start...Lolly, are you OK?" I ask.

"No, Randy, I'm not. I can't believe this happened. I can't do the rest of the show. I'm sorry."

Bursting into tears, she runs out of the tent into Fringe Central.

"I'm sorry, ladies and gentlemen. Sadly, it looks like we're going to have to end the show there. We hope you enjoyed what you did get to see and will tell your friends. Thank you for coming."

It's a sincere speech, and my obvious embarrassment only adds to the authenticity. Stepping outside to say goodbye to our guests as they leave, I'm relieved to see they are all smiling. I am so busy feeling foolish, it never occurs to me our audience might actually enjoy being part of the joke.

I look over and see Lolly in the crowd of Fringe Central with an acquaintance consoling her. She explains to him in great detail how our show was just terrorized by this rogue theater company called Fag Hog. I am quite sure no one will believe this outlandish story until several audience members approach her to offer their sympathies and corroborate her story! The match is tossed, the fire spreads, and the joke is on.

The same thing happens at each performance. We do our show until we have no show, Fag Hog appears, and Lolly bursts into tears and out into Fringe Central. Each time, our little audience is fully complicit. They wander into the crowd never saying much, which is just enough. They have a few fuzzy details about a disruption and a group called Fag Hog.

Our venue manager Dom, on the other hand, enjoys being in on the joke so much, he tells the full story in great detail to anyone who asks. I'm sure he's the one who planted the idea in the heads of another theater troupe that Fag Hog was gunning for them next.

"If those fuckers even try to disrupt our show, I swear I'll take my prop gun and pop them right in the fucking face!" said Bowman, smashing his fist into his hands. The cast of his show, *Fuck You, or Dead Pee Holes,* had an emergency meeting on how to deal with the increasing threat of Fag Hog.

"How do they get in?" a cast member asked Lolly, who they brought in as an unfortunate expert in dealing with the rogue theater company.

"They used to just come in through the front door," she told the silently attentive group. "But Dom has been standing by the door now, so they've taken to coming in through the roof."

"How many times have they disrupted your show?" asked another cast member.

"Every performance. Look, guys, they have a bone to pick with The Beggars Group. I don't think they're going to try and fuck up your show."

Unwilling to reveal the truth, Lolly wanted to ease their minds as much as she could. Even the thought of having their show invaded was disrupting to them.

"Well, if they do, they'll be sorry," Bowman said with conviction to loud cheers from a unified cast. "I'm ready to kick some fucking ass."

This was starting to get out of control. Every time we were at a Fringe Party, or even at a Lower East Side bar, someone would approach us and ask us to recount our tales with our nemesis.

We performed our sixth show without a hitch to another single-digit audience. Lolly assumed her position, crying in Dom's arms in the heart of Fringe Central. This time, however, John, the head of the festival, catches notice and approaches her.

"What happened?" he asks. "Why are you crying?"

"You haven't heard?" Dom asks, and he launches into the whole story.

Within minutes, Lolly, Dickey, and I find ourselves sitting in the FringeNYC offices being drilled by the festival heads, John and Elaina. We had been summoned because they thought we were victims, but we knew in our hearts we were not victims. We were criminals. I was already convinced they were going to shut us down. Just like my fifth-grade jungle gym haunted house.

You see, a little boy named Joey did a headless-horseman bit where he threw a winter coat all the way down the aisle toward the viewer. It was a terrifying final moment for our patrons. Everyone loved it...until the zipper poked the eye of a first-grader, and she cried to the playground monitor. Ms. Ford marched right over and shut us down. I appealed by telling her I'd screen the kids and do the headless-horseman jacket throw for fourth- and fifth-graders only, but she wouldn't hear it. She shut the operation down.

"What are their names?" asks John.

"Becky, Derek, and Tom," Lolly says quickly.

"Why do they hate you?"

"They were supposed to do the Fringe with us. We were all working on a show together, but then we realized they were crazy, so we told them we weren't going to do the festival anymore. When they found out we lied, they got pissed, I guess, and decided to exact revenge."

Our improvisations had perfected this material. We knew it so well, we could complete each other's sentences, which made for a very believable tale. When they asked us what they looked like, we described ourselves. Our subtle attempt to let them in on the joke proved futile. They didn't get it. They were running the largest theater festival in the city and didn't have time to search our answers for subtle nuances.

They held us in their offices for what felt like an eternity. It was mid-August, and we were in the Lower East Side tenements in 90-degree heat with no air circulation. It felt as if it were 100 years earlier, and we were brand-new immigrants smashed into a humid, vent-free boarding house. The interrogation was starting to melt our brains.

Finally, they tell us they're beefing up security throughout Fringe Central and will make sure they have three people by our doors for our final performance.

"Don't forget to put someone one the roof," I say.

"How do they come in through the roof?" they ask.

"Have you seen the roof of our theater? They lift a corner and drop in."

It isn't impossible, but it's certainly improbable. Still, they don't catch the hint. We thank them a million times and leave the office as fast as we can.

It was quite a show. Not one of us blinked.

And that's how we ended up standing in the oppressive sun on Stanton Street with Dickey predicting a death.

"We're terrorists, you know," Dickey said. "We're fucking terrorizing the whole fucking festival."

"We're not terrorists," I said. "Fag Hog are the terrorists."

"*WE'RE FAG HOG!*" Dickey shouted.

He got me on a technicality, but I didn't want to hear it. Nobody wants to be Fag Hog. But Dickey was right. We *were* Fag Hog. With our spectacular performance in the Fringe offices only minutes behind us, I had convinced myself we were innocent.

"We should go back and tell them," Dickey said. "We have to put a stop to this."

"No way," Lolly said. "What is that going to do?"

"Dickey's right, Lolly," I said. "We should go back. They're starting to put some serious resources toward protecting the festival against a fictitious threat. It's kind of like we're shouting 'Fire!' in a crowded theater."

"How are we going to go back in there and tell them we just made all that shit up? I'm not going to do that."

Now, Lolly was right. They did not look as if they were having a very good day, and we just had a million chances to come clean but opted instead to lay thicker hints.

"Why don't we get into our Fag Hog costumes and go in there and introduce ourselves as Fag Hog?" Dickey suggested. "That way, we don't have to ever admit to anything."

It was a stupid idea. A stupid, stupid, stupid idea. And so, we put on our sombreros and ponchos in the sweltering heat and walked back to the office with our tails between our legs.

When we walk into the oppressive former immigrant hellhole of an office, they barely look at us.

"Is everything OK, guys?"

Obviously running a fringe theater festival had rendered them immune to wildly dressed people in the office.

"Everything is fine," Dickey says.

"We're Fag Hog," Lolly says, trying not to laugh. "We heard you wanted to see us."

They don't even take a full second to reply.

"Get out!" is all we hear. We turn around and head home. They aren't interested in wasting any more time on our games.

It was so anti-climatic. Somehow, life is more electrically charged when there's the possibility someone might die. I know it sounds terrible, but isn't that why we watch football and the Indy 500? Our humanity really isn't as polished as we'd like to believe.

We perform our last show as usual, but when we reach the "stopping-the-world moment," we simply stop.

"Thank you all for coming to see our work in progress, *Stopping The World*. That is all the play we have for you at this time. We're going to keep working on it over the next few months with the hope of presenting it later this fall. In the meantime, keep your eyes open for moments that stop your world. The next paradigm shift could be right around the corner."

THE WORLD STOPS

I got off the C train at 50th Street and Eighth Avenue. Running late, I had taken the C train, which arrived first, instead of the B, which dropped me off right below the building where I worked. It was a gorgeous day with not a cloud in the sky, and I wanted to stretch my legs a bit before confining myself to my cubicle.

I stopped at a bodega and ordered a large coffee with milk, no sugar. The man behind the counter, who was listening to the radio, told me an airplane had hit a building downtown. I'd heard once that a plane had flown into the Empire State Building, but that was a long time ago and I found it odd such a thing could happen again. Surely, navigation equipment had improved.

I paid for my coffee, stepped outside, and looked south. I couldn't see the lower Manhattan skyline, but I could see smoke emanating from that direction.

Hurrying to work, I walked the two long avenue blocks to Sixth Avenue in record time. I was trying to beat the clock, but the truth was, it had already won. I was officially five minutes late even before I got to my building.

Because the anchor tenant in my building was Fox News, the lobby's many television screens and tickers endlessly spouted right-wing crap. It was the last news source I would trust, so I always ignored the dazzling displays. Today, however, the lobby was packed with people, all standing in silence staring up at the screens. Resisting the temptation to look myself, lest I be turned to stone by catching a glimpse of Bill O'Reilly, I headed to the elevator. Finally safe on the 19th floor, I reported to my cubicle.

"You know, a plane hit the World Trade Center," said my boss Bob.

"Yeah, I heard, some Cessna or something, right?"

"No, it was an airliner," he said. "You need to call your parents."

And he went back into his office.

I understood the gravity of a jetliner crashing into a building, but I wasn't sure why that warranted a phone call to my parents. Then, a woman I'd never been friendly with ran out of her office and announced that another plane had hit the second tower.

"It's like we're under attack," I said, almost joking. While that was the impression I was getting, it certainly didn't strike me as a reality.

"We are," Bob hollered from his office. "Call your parents!"

I didn't know how to process his intensity, so I did as I was told. I picked up the receiver and phoned home.

"Hello!" said my seven-year-old nephew.

"Hi, Kevin, what are you doing?" I asked.

"Nana's here, and we're watching New York burn."

I was struck by his frank observation while at the same time recognizing how truly terrifying his observation actually was. I was *in* New York, and my nephew was 3,000 miles away watching it burn.

"Can you put Nana on the phone?" I asked.

He handed the phone to my mother, who was at once relieved to hear my voice and terrified by what she was seeing. Having never been to New York, she had no sense of midtown and downtown. All she knew was that planes were hitting buildings in the Financial District, and I worked at a financial institution.

"Get out of there now!" she instructed.

I spent a few minutes unsuccessfully trying to convince her my office was safe. I assured her I would flee to safety should danger come my way.

"Yeah, right," my mom replied. "You can't outrun a plane, Randy."

I couldn't argue with that, so I said I'd leave and hung up. Reality had started to settle in, and I got busy on the phone, trying to connect my coworkers with their loved ones, many of whom were navigating the chaos of the lower Manhattan Streets.

Two hours later, after two more planes had gone down, U.S. airspace was neutralized, and the World

Trade Center was no more. Those of us who hadn't already left the office decided we'd done all we could. Scott was walking up from his 20th Street office. Donna, who was unable to get back to Long Island, and I met him in front of our building on the corner of 48th Street and walked uptown to Scott's apartment on 79th Street and Broadway.

The New York streets were quiet in a way I'd never seen. No horns, no planes, no loud shouting, only crowds of people moving north, away from the destruction. Each time we'd pass an avenue, we looked down at the spire of smoke that, like a volcano, seemed to be endlessly spewing ash.

Chills climbed my spine when I saw the survivors. Unmistakably marked head to toe by a white dusting of ash, their big eyes, glazed over with tears, were wide open, scanning everything in a daze. It was as if they'd been buried for a century and were coming back into the world for a second time, expatriated from the lives they once knew. They were living ghosts.

Scott and I hosted a small group of assorted friends at his apartment until they could all find their way back home. Then, feeling restless, we walked through Central Park. The scene was surreal. The beauty of the day and the silence of the sky created a breathtaking calm. Only the birds spoke, and even they were having a difficult time communicating in the hollow air.

We only had to look south to see the cause of this unusual reality. It was as if, when the buildings fell, they had sucked all the awful, loud, hate out of the air and left peace in its place. To this day, it remains the most serene scene I've ever experienced, right in the middle of one of the busiest cities on earth. We would soon learn that the destruction's gravity was so intense, it pulled several month's worth of awful, loud hate into the ground with it. The fall of 2001 would be the most magical on record. The weather, the people, and the city would be placed in a healing trance.

By the time evening set in, I realized I hadn't actually seen what happened. I was still relying on my imagination to draw what a jetliner hitting the World Trade Center looked like. So, I left Scott, went home, and pulled out the little TV we kept in the closet to watch this universal stopping-the-world moment. And, as the footage rolled on and the stories began to unfold, I experienced my own stopping-the-world moment in the small, curved reflection. What I understood to be my youth had ended.

As the winds shifted, bringing with them the smells of burning metal, The Beggars Group gathered in my apartment to determine our next move. As we were settling in, we heard a story on NPR about a musician who, when the first plane hit, was having a smoke before heading up to his day job at the World Trade Center. He had written a song about his experience and played it on his saxophone. It was Charles, Lolly's former infatuation from The Gold Sparkles. We hadn't heard neither hide nor hair of him since *The Expatriates*, but there he was, on National Public Radio, making his art a week after the tragedy.

"Well, nobody can say we have bad timing," Dickey said.

"We can't do *Stopping the World* now," I said, leaning out the window with my cigarette.

"Why not?" Dickey asked.

"Because it's too...now. It's too much. Doing *Stopping the World* now would be like reading the *Diary of Anne Frank* while the Germans still occupied Holland."

A silent Lolly, who'd had her head in her arms for the last 10 minutes, suddenly looked up.

"We need to do a piece that is the equivalent of giving blood. You know? It has to have that kind of significance."

It was a deadly thought, and I could tell she was lost in the rabbit hole.

"And what would that be, Lolly?" Dickey asked.

"I don't know. It's like we've lost our sense time and place. You know. Like we don't know what day it is, or what month even. I don't know. I feel like we should be doing something that's helpful with that."

She wasn't making sense and retreated back into her folded arms.

"Theater that is the equivalent of giving blood..." I said. "Don't you think that's asking too much from the art form? I mean... I don't know, it seems like we could really set ourselves up for failure there. Trying to be provocative and entertain is a tall enough order. Giving blood... I don't know."

"I'm talking about doing something that important," Lolly said, standing up. "You know. Giving people that feeling."

"No, I don't," I replied.

"You know the feeling you have when you've given blood?"

"No," I replied.

"Haven't you ever given blood?"

"No."

"You've never given blood? Dickey, you know what I'm talking about, right?"

"No," Dickey said.

"You guys have never given blood?"

"No, Lolly, gay men haven't been able to give blood since the '80s," Dickey said.

"That's fucked up," Lolly replied. "Anyway, it feels good, because you're giving a piece of yourself. Life. It's profound."

And she stopped there because she could see we got the point but were no longer going to endure the metaphor. Picking up one of the many magazines strewn on the floor, Lolly began to read. Dickey and I followed suit, and we sat for hours taking turns reading articles and columns that we found funny or profound.

"Why don't we take these articles, and put them together into an evening called *Stopping the World*?" Dickey suggested. "We have a lot of material and all this funny stuff from *The Onion* to keep the show light."

"Like a living newspaper," Lolly said.

"Exactly!" Dickey said. "And they're having a big art night at The Space in a couple of weeks. I'll bet they'd let us do it there."

"Oh, you've got to be kidding," I said. "It's a great idea, Dickey, but The Space?"

"It will be good, Randy Anderson. We'll talk about what everyone is thinking about in a theatrical setting, where people can share in their fears, and hopes, and what-ever else they're experiencing."

"And it's all found text from current newspaper and magazine articles," Lolly said, jumping to life for the first time in hours.

"I love the idea, but The Space?" I was outnumbered.

Two weeks later, we arrived at The Space on a clear, crisp night. The Empire State Building was perfectly framed in the large factory windows. The whole place was already crawling with poor, smelly artists. The politicians' jars must have been overflowing.

We hadn't been out to The Space since our *Do It!* production, and we noticed absolutely nothing had changed. Apparently, we were the only people who bothered to clean anything. The energy was frenetic, but I couldn't tell why. Was it because of all the funky art? Or was evil still present? I became nervous about being vulnerable in this environment. We spent a half-hour wandering the galleries, analyzing art, and striking up conversations with smelly artists, killing time before our 8 o'clock curtain.

I don't know exactly where the rumor came from or who started it. Maybe the evil presence got the ball rolling, but all I know is Lolly came up to me and said she had heard the Empire State Building had been attacked.

"We can see it from the western windows," I said. "I saw it when we came in."

We ran over to the room with the windows to the west. And there, framed in the giant factory windows, was nothing.

"Holy shit!" Lolly said. "It's gone."

"It's gone," I repeated.

We ran to find Dickey. He'd already heard about the attack from someone else and was frantically searching for anyone who might have a radio or more information. We found Fannie and Harrison and gave them the update. We were genuinely scared, and our panic grew with each minute.

"How is it that none of these art projects is a radio?" I asked. There were Barbie installations, "yarn art," collections of matchbox cars, so I could only assume there was a working radio glued to a cat somewhere.

"This is an art gallery, Randy, not a science fair," said Fannie as we continued running through the space, informing everyone we knew about the tragedy.

Most of the artists listened to our story about the vanishing building with curiosity but only moderate interest and certainly no alarm. It was only then that I began to sense the many kinds of drugs pulsing through The Space. Everyone was too hopped up on whatever to care that our city had been attacked yet again. After 10 minutes of searching for any kind of communicative device, we grew fearful we'd be trapped in Queens...and that we'd be stuck at The Space, a fate worse than death.

Our panic escalated. We started running from room to room announcing that terrorists were dismantling our skyline. The drugged-out, smelly artists just looked at us in unexplainably funny ways. Some laughed and went back to what they were doing. Others began following us around until we had a parade of people moving from room to room. Finally, we assembled in the common lobby where we made the decision to save ourselves.

"We're fucking out of here!" Lolly shouted to the room, and we descended the stairs and went out to the street. We were absolutely out of our minds, talking a mile a minute about the terrible the energy at The Space and how we prayed we'd make it back to Manhattan when we ran into Scott at the subway entrance.

"Thank God, you're OK," I said, giving him a hug.

"Of course, I am, why wouldn't I be?" he asked. "And why aren't you guys at The Space getting ready for your show?"

"The Empire State Building has been bombed," I said, and everyone else jumped in with all the details we'd conjured up in our minds. Scott held his hands out in an attempt to slow us down.

"You guys, I was just at 34th Street. There wasn't any bomb. The building is still there. Look!" He pointed over the rooftops.

Sure enough, there was the Empire State Building slowly being revealed by the passing cloud.

"So...shit," I said. "Wow."

"Should we go back?" Dickey asked.

"You guys gotta do the show," said Scott. "I came all the way out here."

"I don't know," said Lolly sheepishly. "I don't think we can go back up there after the way we left."

It was true. We had made a pretty big fuss about a terrorist attack.

"Well, I'm not going back," I said. "That place is messed up. There is nothing but bad energy in that space. Every time we're in there, something bad happens. I hate it, and I never want to go back there ever again."

Nobody wanted to argue with that, so we got on the N train and got the fuck out of Queens.

We heard later that our "performance" was very well-received. The smelly artists and their friends were all impressed with our acting and thought the interactivity was a nice touch. They really liked how we commented on the new culture of fear in our society but would have picked a less obvious target for our fake terrorist attack.

The artists all agreed that performing throughout the entire gallery was spectacular. These were, after all, people who didn't like to sit in one place for very long. And while they all understood our piece had to end with us leaving the building, they wished we had come back for a curtain call.

The Space debacle wasn't merely a stumbling block, it was a sign we had fallen flat on our faces. We were struggling with how best to serve our audience, ourselves, and our craft. For the past two years, we had produced over a dozen shows and at least a dozen more single-night events. We were always working on two or more projects at a time, with another three in the pipeline. Ideas seemed to flow effortlessly.

But now, we had nothing. No ideas, no projects, no prospects. It was a head-on collision, 60 to zero in one second. Our collective concussion was severe.

"I think I'm gonna paint that wall," Lolly said one afternoon staring at the longest wall in our living room.

"Just as long as you don't paint over my footprints," I said, referring to the blue footprints running parallel to the floor across another wall. It was a late-night project of Big Rob's and mine. I dipped my feet into the paint and he lifted me as I walked them across the wall. It was no easy feat, and I was very proud of the work.

"Don't worry, I won't."

I watched for a while as she drew orange lines in random patterns. Then, she'd work in some gray highlights. Eventually, I got inspired and, after a trip to the bodega for a six-pack, began working on my own wall. We worked through the night. The colors were erratic and the designs chaotic, but the room burst to life in a way we'd never thought possible. It was warm and inviting, even though one of my paintings was a series of explosions.

"We should do a show here," I said, looking around at the oranges, blues, and grays.

"Here?" Lolly asked.

"Yeah, nothing crazy...a reading, or an evening of music. Something about the room feels safe, like a coffee shop in Amsterdam."

"Of course, you'd feel safe in an Amsterdam coffee shop."

"Well, maybe 'warm' is the word I'm looking for."

"No, 'safe' is the right word. It feels safe."

The following Saturday, we produced a reading in our living room. We invited a friend to read a story she'd been working on and asked Jay to play an acoustic guitar score behind it. We bought some track lighting and a dimmer for the "stage," carved some jack-o' lanterns, filled the room with wine and baked goods, and invited everyone we knew. Nobody declined.

That evening was the theatrical equivalent of giving blood. With all that had happened and all that was happening, people simply wanted to come together. And we'd created a safe space where they could do just that. They entered, and we took their coats. They ate homemade apple pie and banana bread while chatting with strangers. Then, we all sat down, drank wine, and listened, like children, to a story, safe in the flickering lights of an indisputable October.

HOME

For those who know or those who just happen to be there, the show starts in the bar across the street from 85 East Fourth Street. There at around 7 p.m., you find a Frenchman and an Englishman bickering about the endless subjects a Frenchman and an Englishman can bicker about. Never raising their voices, their arguments are playful yet permanent. After finishing five beers between the two of them (the fifth being consumed by the winner of that day's wager), they walk across a bone-dry street under the giant domes of their doorman umbrellas and enter the Kraine Theatre.

It is the spring of 2002, and this is the beginning of *The Expatriates*, the final movement in The Beggars Group's second act.

The struggle to generate work had become intense during the winter leading us into 2002. The only thing we'd done since the October reading was *More Making Out in Japanese*, a silly "sex seminar" play based on a travel guide. The world had changed so drastically, we were unable to regain our footing. Desperate to see the world as we had before, we reached for those familiar foreigners, *The Expatriates*, to help guide us home. We must have understood on some level this would mean the end. We had to. Why else would we have constructed the play we did?

By the time our two porters arrive in the lobby, it's crowded with patrons. Noj, playing the Frenchman, cheerfully ushers the first party into the theater, holding his umbrella over their heads. The houselights are dim, and the sounds of a rainstorm fill the space. A quilted curtain, made of found fabric just thin enough to see through the threads, hangs in front of the stage. In the center of the curtain, we project the word HOME.

Noj discourages the patrons from taking their dark, storm-swept seats and leads them through the curtain, into the light, to the onstage café, complete with several small tables and complimentary wine at the bar. Dickey, our bartender, hands them each a program and offers them a drink. Patrons either stand or sit with their drinks and eventually notice a table with two seated people who don't quite look like fellow audience members. It's F. Scott Fitzgerald and Dorothy Parker, quietly chatting. Are they having an affair?

We wanted to re-create the play from the ground up, so we brought in performers we could trust, people who would bring as much to the play as they would to their performances. Harrison would reprise his role as

Scott, I would play George, Lolly would play Zelda, Jenny would return as Dorothy Parker, and we invited Kevin to tackle the role of Ernest Hemingway. It is, for our company, an all-star lineup.

By 8:05 p.m., the Kraine stage buzzes with mingling audience members while others move to the house to secure a good seat. Ernest Hemingway and Zelda join Dorothy and Scott, and their conversation is no longer quiet.

Zelda's growing erratic behavior cues Dickey to usher the rest of the audience offstage and into their seats. Dickey gets a look of disgust in his eyes every time he gazes Zelda's way. He truly dislikes this person, and she truly doesn't care. And nobody is acting.

We wanted the play to begin in as "artificial" a place as possible. To us, that meant creating as real an environment as possible, a hyper-pretend world. The goal was to try too hard so it would look fake. But it didn't read fake to our audience. To them, the whole experience was quite unique, magical, and real.

We set up this construct for one very specific reason: to destroy it. The whole show would fall apart, decay if you will, to our end point—as "real" a place as possible, which actually turns out to feel very artificial. We are going to show the destruction of our characters' lives in the play, as we'd done before, but then we are going to destroy the construct of the play, then the actual script, and then the entire company of players.

By the end of the evening, all the magic of being in the south of France with famous authors will dissipate. The storytellers, known as The Beggars Group, will be gone. Every layer of performance will be peeled away, and we'll all be left with only ourselves. Performers and audience members will become a bunch of bodies in a room. It is a theatrical suicide mission.

Once all the audience members settle in their seats, we hear a crash of thunder, the lights go down, and the curtain falls on a dark stage. Much like the first version of *The Expatriates*, the opening 15 minutes is a well-made play. Topical dialogue between interesting characters establishes time, place, and situations. The situation this time isn't Zelda's ballet-dancing, nor is it the book she wrote. This time, the play is about Zelda's going crazy.

One stormy evening, Ernest, Dorothy, and Scott discuss her dissolving state while sitting in a cottage somewhere in the south of France. Zelda, after almost causing Scott to crash the car on the way back from the café, runs off into the storm and is nowhere to be found.

Our inferences are not subtle. Everyone knows people who run out into a storm are crazy. King Lear is the most obvious example. But our audience, too, had fled into the rain just before the show began. Harrison, who had deftly written and constructed the scene, would have kept going and seen the play through if Lolly hadn't demanded that he stop.

"I don't want this to be just another fucking play!" she had screamed in the middle of rehearsal. "It needs to dissolve. Deteriorate. Decompose. It's all fake if it doesn't decompose."

We were all used to disagreeing in rehearsals, and nobody was a stranger to Lolly's conceptual outbursts, but something about her tone was very different. She was mean, loud, and a bit grotesque—which was oddly familiar to us. We'd written this person before.

"But we can do that with the script!" Harrison said. "I can make that happen with the script."

"No, you can't!" Lolly countered. "Because there is a script! We're not going to have a script by the end of this play. The play itself will have dissolved into nothing. Into shards of pulp."

"I'm not interested in that," Harrison said.

"Well, I'm not interested in doing your fake-piece-of-crap script."

"What are you talking about?" I interjected. "It's a good script!"

"It's crap!" Lolly said. "You got the balls to destroy your own words, Harry?"

By this time, Harrison realized he had two choices: He could punch her in the face or take a walk around the block. We weren't watching Lolly and Harrison. This was Zelda and Scott, and Harrison hadn't signed up for a method-acting developmental session.

Thankfully, he chose to walk around the block.

That was only the beginning of the fights. While the play rotted away, so did our rehearsals. What we were putting on stage began happening in real life, which was what we wanted to do, and it was oddly brilliant. But the fact that Lolly and Zelda were becoming the same person, and that person was going crazy, meant we all had to deal with her. And crazy people are neither fun nor easy to deal with.

Back in our play, Zelda enters the stage in typical Zelda fashion, soaking wet from the storm and excited by something she'd just experienced.

"Scott, the most amazing thing has happened. I met a man at the café. An amazing man. A prophet, Scott. A prophet. Oh, God, baby, I am so happy. I don't even know where to begin."

Her insanity starts in a place of excited beauty. Then, lightning and thunder. Zelda, in her excitement, faints, and the power goes out. Another thunderclap, and the door opens to reveal a stranger from beyond, George Antheil. Still the ringleader of the production, my character now has a more subtle control over the events. He no longer abruptly stops the action but guides it from one place to another.

After a moment, Zelda awakens, delighted to see George. She explains that the beauty of his music had caused her to overexcite, and she implores George to play this magical music for the others. I call forth my musicians, who enter carrying electric guitars—the first crack in our set-up world.

The band, A Brief View of the Hudson, blends country, folk, and rock. They set down their amplifiers center stage and sit on them. Nobody can pretend we are in the 1920s any more. And with the first riff of the guitar, the chaos begins and doesn't stop until the end of the play. The deconstruction is unstoppable.

Lolly's behavior in the rehearsal room had continued to grow stranger and more unbearable. But unlike the first production of *The Expatriates*, she wasn't the director, so she got a lot more pushback. We had cast out any notion of a director, and people didn't have to do what she told them. Building a consensus was not easy, especially for Lolly's strong will, and the more resistance she felt, the more frustrated she became; and the more she behaved badly, the more she created resistance.

Eventually, Kevin, Jenny, Harrison, and I put on our kid gloves when dealing with Lolly. We pressed forward with the work, but the entire cast made it very clear to me they would not be working with The Beggars Group again—not so long as Lolly was involved. I'd seen it coming, and I was fully complicit. Once again, the company was falling apart, and once again it was because Lolly was too aggressive and I was too passive.

The nightmare in the play's second half is loud. With the electric guitars at full volume, Dorothy Parker's howling horrors are creepier and more threatening than ever. Hemingway's solitary speeches are more heartbreakingly devoid of hope. And F. Scott and Zelda's fights are, quite simply, real.

Since we were writing this during rehearsals when everyone was feeling awful about the show, the hatred and despair permeate every word. It is a horror-show collection of scenes, each shorter and louder than the one before. We are, in a way, seeing the world of our characters through the eyes of Zelda, and the crazier she gets, the more bizarre and fragmented the scenes become. The narrative fractures at an increasing pace. The play falls apart. Finally, we throw a kicking, screaming Zelda into the asylum.

"I'm going to take a year off from The Beggars Group," I told Lolly one day during the run. "I need to do my own thing for a while. I need a break from this intense collaboration. I'm gonna write a one-man show."

"OK," Lolly responded.

"You can keep the company going if you want."

"I'm not going to do that," she said simply.

This marked the end of our collaboration. It was clean and devoid of feelings. We had an unspoken agreement to leave feelings out of the business of making theater.

The remaining conversation contained few words but tremendous amounts of emotion. In three short years, we'd been generating theater nonstop. Together, we'd burned megawatts of our youthful energy to illuminate the world through art. And we sat in silence, looking back as if we both knew we were making off with something special. Nothing tangible, of course, but we were making off with something. A memory, an awareness, maybe it was just a strong sense of accomplishment. It was something for sure. We recognized ceremony and went through the motions of mourning. I would truly mourn the loss of our collaboration years later but, at the time, I needed to separate myself from the intensity we'd created.

We carry Zelda across the stage and throw her into a chair. Hit her. Drug her. Torture her with words. This was how crazy people were treated in the 1920s. And this is how we all feel now about Lolly. It also happens to be the unpleasant business of decay, the foul-smelling, putrid texture of life disappearing. Now, there are no more scenes. We see only pieces of scenes, which appear in a haphazard fashion.

Then, we start forgetting lines, not having lines, not knowing what character we're playing. The music is the only constant. Everything else on stage is an utter mess. Finally, we are all sitting in a row of chairs facing the audience. The company of players emerges. It's us, The Beggars Group. Wigs have fallen off, costumes aren't on right, the work lights illuminate. We are exposed and breathing heavy in the unforgiving fluorescents. We look at the people. They look at us. Everyone is uncomfortable. But the show doesn't end until the company dissolves.

Kevin exits first, and Jenny quickly follows. They stand and walk up the aisle to the back of the house. I shake my head and exit next, leaving Lolly and Harrison alone on stage for what feels like hours. They can't stand each other in real life, and it's difficult to watch them sit so close. They smell and are ugly to look at.

Finally, Harrison tells her to "fuck off," and she laughs. He leaves the stage.

Lolly, now alone, looks up to that spot where the word *HOME* had been projected on the curtain an hour earlier. It's not there now. We are expatriated. We can no longer go home. There is no home to go to. We now have to keep moving beyond our borders, forever exploring foreign territory. The company we once knew finally rots away, giving its energy to other purposes.

Crouching in the aisle at the back of the house, I watch Lolly try desperately to just "be" with the audience—a task at which she fails miserably. There is too much "real" happening in her. She was filling the room with an intense energy...an inescapable energy that demands attention, reaction.

Like the beggar I saw on the street years ago, she casts out a cloud of dust that covers everyone in the room. I watch the audience shift uncomfortably in their seats, praying for the moment to be over so they can start clapping, standing, something. They are experiencing something intense. It is the strongest reaction we've ever garnered from an audience. It is the beggar effect.

Finally, the lights go down, and the audience applauds. We take our final bows and leave the theater. We know The Beggars Group had a good run, but it's time to take a break to recharge, refocus, and, most importantly, re-imagine the next parts of our lives.

Standing there on East Fourth Street in my black peacoat, taking the last drags off my cigarette, I noticed a man sitting down in the gutter between two cars. By his appearance, I assumed he was either homeless or extremely poor. I stamped out my cigarette and walked toward him, pulling five dollars from my wallet. It was a spontaneous and sudden decision, but one filled with the utmost conviction.

"Randy, are you coming in?" asked Harrison, who was already halfway in the bar.

"Yeah," I stopped and looked toward the bar. "Just a second, I want to..."

"What?" said Harrison, in his most sarcastic tone. "Throw that five dollars in the trash?"

Struck by the insensitivity of his comment, I didn't let it deter me. I turned back around, determined to give this beggar five bucks. The first five had bought me three years of happiness. I was eager to buy another. But, as I turned and bent down to hand the beggar my bill, I realized it was not a person. It was a small stack of garbage bags that only appeared to be a man slumped over in defeat.

I chuckled at myself and headed to the bar. My five dollars was going to buy me a beer, my imagination would provide the happiness. Because by now I knew, if you can imagine it, you can live it. You can make off with any kind of life you want.

THE END

ABOUT THE AUTHOR

Randy Anderson is a performer, producer, and playwright. He founded The Beggars Group in 1999. He has produced over two dozen productions including; *The Expatriates, Do It!,* and *Theadora, She Bitch of Byzantium.* Plays he's written include; *New Year's Resolutions, Homlessness Homosexuals and Heretics, Testing Average, Kill The President, Armor of Wills, and The Dwelling.*

7915722R0

Made in the USA
Charleston, SC
21 April 2011